BWANA KIDOGO

Scenes from a Colonial Childhood

By Chris Durrant

Copyright © 2018 Chris Durrant
Cover design by Lara Juriansz
The moral right of the authors has been asserted
ISBN 978-0-9870637-4-8

Contents

Introduction

Setting the scene

It is a fact that millions of people around the world rejoiced the day I was born. This is not to say that more than a very small number of them were aware (and even fewer would have cared) that my mother had been brought to bed with her first child in the military hospital of the little hill station of Wellington in the Nilgiri Hills, South India. August 15th 1945 marked the end of the Second World War, when the atomic bombs dropped several days before on Nagasaki and Hiroshima had persuaded Japan to sue unconditionally for peace. Six years of killing, brutality, starvation and inhumanity were officially at an end; cause enough for rejoicing even, perhaps, if you were not on the winning side. Cynics may have doubted that this war would be any more effective in ending all wars than had the previous global struggle 25 years before, and how right they were, but for most the relief and joy of the moment must have been overwhelming. Certainly, for Oliver and Cynthia Durrant, the birth of their first son must have seemed the icing on the cake and a symbol of hope and new beginnings in the world of peace that perhaps lay before them.

The photographic record shows that I was no more nor less Churchillian than the average baby. However, at some stage I apparently resembled a cartoon character in the Daily Sketch who had a round head, quite bald except for one curly hair, and consequently became known after him as Pop, a nickname which lasted in close family circles well into my teenage years. I remember nothing at all of India, my home for the first year of my life. With the coming of independence for India and the traumatic Partition of the country into Hindu India and Muslim Pakistan, my father resolved to retire from the Indian Army, with which he had served for the best part of three decades, and try his fortunes in Kenya. And so, shortly before my first birthday, we left the land of my birth, Pa to Kenya to establish himself, and Ma and I to England to await the birth of my brother Tony and to enjoy the coldest British winter that century

.The author, about the time we went to Kenya

I am not quite sure why my parents picked Kenya as their new home. Perhaps they succumbed to the blandishments of the British Government, keen to develop the relatively untouched natural resources of their Colony, and to also get demobilised soldiers off their hands. Another factor was probably the presence there of my Aunt Alice. Married just before the war to her second cousin Raymond (RAT) Clegg-Hill, she was widowed by a German sniper's bullet in the last few weeks of the war in Europe, and went out to run the family farm, "Moya Drift", near Nyeri in view of Mount Kenya. Whatever the reason, Pa arrived in the Colony at the end of 1946 and purchased an orchard property, with a house on it, just beyond Limuru, high in the tea country some 25 miles from the capital, Nairobi. A few months after Tony's birth in May 1947, Ma, Tony and I enjoyed the dubious comforts of the converted troopship, SS "Orbeta" as she steamed along the Med, through the Suez Canal, down the Red Sea and eventually into the gateway of our new home country, the old Arab port of Mombasa.

Chapter 1

Mapsedge, Limuru

The name of our property at Limuru, "Mapsedge", seemed entirely descriptive of its position to a small child with a very literal mind. I could not imagine what, if anything, lay beyond the large meadow behind our house. The house itself was situated near the top of a hillside sloping down into a forested valley. The property was surrounded by wattle trees, with a double row of dark pines between the house and the drive. Much of the land was planted to fruit-trees, mainly plums (Satsumas and Victorias), with some peaches and pears. The house was a weatherboard structure, raised on stumps at the front, with brick chimneys. Limuru, at an altitude of over 7,000 feet, got very chilly at night, and we had a fire most evenings. The nursery, where we had our meals and played, was separated from the main building by a short, covered boardwalk. It had its own little kitchen where Ma used to stew and bottle fruit, and a spare bedroom at the end for guests. Its windows looked out over the small lawn in front of the house, across the orchard and down into the valley where, on frosty mornings, the mist would swirl among the treetops, or sometimes lie like a snowy blanket over the forest. I can remember standing at the window on my 4th birthday and gazing out with pride and satisfaction. Four years old! It seemed a very good age!

Family group at Mapsedge 1947

Junior transport 1949

Although bush living in Kenya at that time was often rather primitive, at Mapsedge we had most modern conveniences. Power was originally provided by a generator, but we eventually joined the mains supply, and we certainly had a telephone by the time we left in 1952. Water was derived from the rain, collected from the roof into a huge concrete tank. Limuru was a high rainfall area, so there was little danger of a drought. Some of our neighbours drew water from the stream in the valley by means of a ram pump which used the power of the stream's flow to force water up a pipe to the storage tank high up on the hillside.

There were two other properties on our side of the hill, one belonging to a Mr Ford who, we believed, owned a big department store in Nairobi (actually, I think he was merely the manager), and the other to another retired military couple, Major "Kink" McKinstry and his wife Cara. "Kink" I remember as an irascible old curmudgeon, with a white bristly moustache and a gruff manner, but Cara was a dear and became a good friend to my mother. They had a grown-up daughter, Hazel, who lived in Uganda and used to visit occasionally.

The establishment at Mapsedge was not, of course, confined to my parents, Tony and me. We had what was regarded in those days as quite a modest staff of retainers, most of whom lived in huts on the property. Apart from the labourers who helped in the orchard there was a *shamba*-boy (gardener), *mpishi* (cook) and one or two houseboys, who cleaned, served at meals and did various household chores. There was also usually a kitchen *toto*, a young lad who made the fires, ran errands, and did sundry other tasks for *mpishi*. When Tony and I were little there was also an ayah in whose company we spent most of the day. We had several ayahs (for some reason they never seemed to last very long!), some Seychelloise, some African. The one I remember best was a jolly Kikuyu lady called Fat Maria. She was a kind, motherly person with a great sense of humour and a wide circle of friends with whom she would spend much of the day gossiping while we played.

It was while sitting with Maria and her coterie at the corner of the road outside our house that I first came across the African way of dealing with pain. A man on a bicycle came pelting down the hill while we were there, far too fast to take the sharp corner at the bottom, where he came to grief with a screech and a clatter and a big cloud of dust. Not surprisingly, he suffered very considerable grazes and cuts and a good deal of blood showed startlingly red against his black skin (their blood is the same colour as ours, Mummy!). The response of the onlookers, to a man and woman, was to roar with laughter. This did not indicate any lack of sympathy or compassion but was just an instinctive reaction to pain or discomfort. I experienced this reflex myself not long afterwards when I was hanging around with the servants outside the kitchen. I was playing with the axe that was used to split wood for the fire, a large and extremely sharp implement that I could hardly lift. Suddenly everybody began laughing, and when I asked what was funny, the *shamba*-boy pointed to my foot. I had let the axe fall on my foot and it had made a deep cut in the top near my toes. The scar is there to this day! Needless to say, once the initial surge of laughter had died away there was much sympathetic clucking and "sorry, *bwana kidogo*, (little master), sorry" as if the accident had been their fault. Maria applied love and antiseptic in equal proportions, and by the time it was necessary to break the news to Ma, it did not seem worth making much of a fuss over.

Many years later, I saw another example of this peculiar African reaction to pain when I was with the school cadets on our annual camp. The climax was a night in the jungle on the upper slopes of Mount Kenya, where we had to bivouac in the bush. We had assigned to us some rangers from the Game Department to make sure that we didn't get lost or trodden on by anything heavy such as a rhino or an elephant. Round the campfire that night, the rangers were regaling us with tales (no doubt well spiced) of their adventures with animals. One man told us of an occasion when he had been mauled by a wounded lion. It must have been an agonising and terrifying experience, and one which had left him with dreadful scars over much of his body. When he came to the gory parts, he could hardly speak he was laughing so much, and as for his mates, they were quite literally rolling on the ground holding their sides.

Between European employer and African servant there often existed in those days an almost feudal bond that was much more than the mere employer-employee relationship. Wages were commonly not only in the form of cash: most employers would provide accommodation for their staff on the premises, and often part of the pay was in kind, for example in food staples such as posho (mealie-meal), sugar and tea. Many employers would help with school expenses or clothing for their servants' children, and in rural areas, a farmer would often have a clinic or even a school for the use of his employees and their families. For the servant, his employer was often "his mother and his father" to whom he could turn for help, advice and succour in time of trouble, while on the other hand there was an expectation on the part of the bwana of loyalty and support well beyond the mere contract to supply labour. I believe that this is why the Mau Mau uprising had an impact on the European population of Kenya out of proportion to the actual terror caused (although that was admittedly considerable) and the number of whites murdered (which was actually fairly small). But more of that later!

Being Africa, there were some disagreeable aspects of our environment. Going barefoot on the grass could make you vulnerable to the invasion of jiggers. The jigger was a small creature that burrowed in through your skin and laid its eggs in a sac beneath the surface. The sac had then to be removed, painfully, with a sterilised hot needle. We were consequently forbidden from going barefoot, a stricture which, as we grew older, we increasingly disregarded. Another less than friendly denizen of the country was *siafu*, the safari ant. These extraordinary creatures would march across the countryside in swarming red columns, literally eating alive anything unlucky enough to get trapped in their way. Poultry were especially vulnerable, and people would commonly keep their chickens in coops raised on stilts standing in cans of water or kerosene to keep siafu at bay. If you trod in a column or, as I once did, fell off your tri-cycle into grass beneath which they were lurking, the ants would swarm up your body with astonishing speed, biting savagely as they went. There was nothing to be done but strip all your clothes off and pick the biting soldier ants off one by one. Mosquitoes, at least malarial ones, were not a problem in Limuru, probably because of the cold and the altitude, and though there were doubtless plenty of snakes about we never saw any. The forest at the bottom of the valley no doubt concealed bigger game, including duiker, bushbuck, and leopard whose spoor we could see on the paths leading to the stream. Leopards are shy and nocturnal, and we never saw one, but the disappearance of two pet dogs and one cat was attributed to leopards, and with some justification: leopards are notoriously partial to dogs. Walking in a patch of forest beyond the McKinstry's house, we would see a troupe of Colobus, perhaps the most beautiful of all the East African monkeys. With their long fringed black and white coats and tufted tails dangling, they would swing effortlessly through the treetops thirty or forty feet above us while we watched, bewitched by their beauty. Once, on the McKinstry's lawn, I found a bush-baby, quite dead, its huge eyes closed and its soft grey fur damp with the morning dew, and marvelled at its tiny black hands, so astonishingly human.

There was, of course, no shortage of domestic animals. In the early years we had two dogs, Shem and Ham, genial hounds of indeterminate ancestry who, as mentioned above, probably found their way to doggy heaven via a leopard's dinner table. They were replaced, towards the end of our time at *Limuru,* by a canine "Odd Couple" who greatly endeared themselves to all who knew them. "Titus" was an Airedale, a large and, because my parents never bothered to keep him appropriately clipped, shaggy dog, of a very amiable disposition and absolutely no brain at all. In his later years he developed the belief that he was a lap-dog, a delusion in which he received, needless to say, no encouragement from the family. I recall an occasion when one of my mother's Guiding colleagues was visiting for afternoon tea, a somewhat nervous Indian lady who was, as it turned out, allergic to dogs. Her distress when Titus took a fancy to her and tried to climb onto her lap can well be imagined!

The other half of this comic duo, the Ronnie Corbett to Titus's

Barker, was a Sealyham named, like all of his litter, after a prominent local jockey, in his case Arthur Lister. Lister was seldom called by his proper name, however, except by Pa, who had a taste for formality, or when he had done something especially vile. Otherwise, he was known, for some reason I cannot now remember, as "Mr.Bloggs" or "Bloggs" for short. Titus and Bloggs, despite the disparity in their size and breeds, became firm friends, and were much-loved members of our entourage for many years.

Ma was essentially a cat person, and we always had cats in the household. The earliest I recall was a handsome marmalade tom named, like so many pets of that era, "Winston". There was also "Buggins", a dignified tabby and, most memorably, "Mittens". Mittens was my mother's special cat, a Seal Point Siamese, delicate and elegant in all respects except her voice, which was the typical Siamese raucous yowl. Like most Siamese, she was capable of great affection and adored Ma. Also typical of her breed, she had eclectic tastes in food, and would sit on the arm of my mother's chair at tea-time, her lovely triangular face and deep blue eyes following each morsel of cake or sandwich on its journey from the plate to Ma's mouth until she could stand it no more and a delicate chocolate paw would be put out to arrest the hand as if to say "Excuse me! Could it be that you have forgotten me?" Mittens had several litters, the first of which, as so often happens, was conceived out of (official) wedlock as a result of an encounter with some vagrant feline Flynn. One of this litter, an all-black kitten, we kept, and he became my personal cat. He was named "Pinkle-purr" after A. A. Milne ("Pink" for short) and he inherited his mother's voice and sweet nature though, unfortunately, his father's independence.

'Mittens' and CD at Mapsedge 1951

We always seemed to have people staying at Mapsedge, and indeed the record, in the form of the Visitors' Book, does show a steady stream of guests. Most of these were family, including my Aunt Alice and her son David, two months my junior, who were still living at Moya Drift Farm at Mweiga near Mount Kenya. My mother's younger brother, Peter Chapman, was also in Kenya. A soldier with the Greenjackets, he had been seconded just after the war to the 5th King's African Rifles (KAR) stationed at that time at Langata near Nairobi. Later retiring from the army with the rank of Lieutenant-Colonel, he joined the Kenya Police and served for many years at Nakuru, in the Rift Valley some 100 miles north-west of Nairobi. He and his lovely wife, Peggie, were frequent visitors, together with their little daughter, Judy. On one occasion, Uncle Peter was our guest on his own, having come down to Nairobi to have all his teeth out, apparently a not uncommon solution to dental problems in those days. On his return from the dentist the poor man lay in the darkened guest room at the end of the nursery while we children were strictly enjoined to keep well away from the area as "Uncle Peter is not well". Poor fellow, it must have been agony. My grandmother, Dorothy Chapman, was another whose name features prominently in the Visitors' Book, as does the old family nannie, Jessie Brooker, known, for reasons that were less apparent in her mellow old age when we knew her, as "No No Nannie".

Air transport was just starting to become the norm for travellers between East Africa and Europe. When Ma, Tony, and I went out to Kenya for the first time in late 1947 we came by sea, but by the 1950s more and more people were going by air. Much of the early passenger air travel was by flying boat, and I can remember meeting an aunt from England at Lake Naivasha, a freshwater lake in the Rift Valley about 50 miles from Nairobi. We heard the deep drone in the distance and then the massive Sunderland flying-boat appeared low in the northern sky and circled briefly before dipping down and settling heavily on the water in a sheet of spray like a fat goose. The flying-boat has always struck me as a very civilised way to travel, combining much of the comfort and relaxation of an ocean liner with something of the convenience of a conventional aeroplane. They were not very fast and did not fly high, so passengers had a chance to see something of the countryside they were flying over and to adjust to the changes in the climate and the time-zone. On the way out from England they landed several times on the Nile, at Cairo and Khartoum, where the passengers would disembark for the night. The trip from Southampton to the Rift Valley Lakes took a number of days, and although this was an improvement on the sea voyage which took weeks, it was bound to lose out to land-borne aircraft, which could do the journey, even then, in a couple of days.

I had, in those days, a plentiful supply of aunts, most of them my father's sisters. His favourite, of whom we were also very fond, was Aunt Faith, only a few years his senior. Faith was a tallish, thinnish, slightly mannish figure with neatly-permed grey hair and the distinctive Durrant nose. She had never married and lived out her last years in genteel poverty in lodgings in Camberley, Surrey. After her death in 1968 it transpired that she had been quite well off, a fact of which she had either been unaware or had, through some ingrained habit of thrift, been unwilling to use for the purpose of improving her own standard of living. Faith had a great sense of humour, very like her younger brother's, and a penchant for Fox's Glacier Mints. She also liked a little 'nip' of Guiness, poured from a tiny brown bottle, as a night-cap. On the other side of the family, of course, we had my mother's sister, Alice, known by us in later years as the "Kali Aunt". *Kali* is a splendid Kiswahili word meaning 'sharp' (as of a knife) or 'fierce' or 'angry'. Any and all of these meanings were suitable for Alice from time to time, and we were much in awe of her. In her old age she allowed the kind heart that was always there to rise much closer to the surface, though she was still quite capable of wielding an acid tongue and did not suffer fools gladly.

Although most of the visitors were relatives of one sort or another, there were some who were not. One such was Mollie Woldringh. Mollie was either a widow or a divorcee (not the sort of question children asked in those days) and had been married at least twice, most recently to a Dutchman named Woldringh. Her child by an earlier marriage, Diana Dudley-Taylor, then at school at the Kenya High School in Nairobi, was also a regular visitor. Mollie stands out in my mind for the immense collection of pills which she kept in a special cabinet in her bedroom. She was undoubtedly not a well lady, but she certainly made the most of her ailments and her stock of remedies would have put the average pharmacy to shame. I was particularly interested in a large jar of delicious-looking brown pills. In my limited experience, anything that colour had to taste of chocolate, which I adored, so I awaited my chance, slipped into her room when no-one was about, and helped myself to a large handful of the chocolate drops. To my dismay, they turned out to be quite revolting, bitter and metallic. It was a salutary experience. I have never been that keen on pills since.

Fairly early on in our time at Limuru, it became evident that pension plus fruit sales were not going to equal a reasonable standard of living, and Pa got an administrative job with the Kenya Police Reserve (KPR). This obliged him to drive into Nairobi every day, only a distance of about 26 miles but, given the state of most of the roads in Kenya in those days, quite a substantial journey. Very few roads outside the main towns of Nairobi, Mombasa and Nakuru were tarred. The road down the escarpment into the Rift Valley, constructed by Italian prisoners of war during the recent conflict, was one, and there was an absurd couple of miles of tarmac at a place called Mackinnon Road on the way to Mombasa, where British troops had been stationed during the war. Otherwise, however, motorists had to put up with roads made, at best, of the red lateritic murram that was the standard road base or else simply compacted red or black soil.

The task of keeping these roads in a passable state at all times was clearly beyond the capacity of the Public Works Department (PWD – standing, so the cynics said, for "Potholes Widened and Deepened"). When dry, these roads developed bone-jarring corrugations and cavernous potholes, the latter often concealed by a filling of fine dust so that the unwary driver would not see them until his wheel crashed down into the pit, often causing havoc with suspension or tyres. During the rains, the roads would turn into a sea of mud, requiring great skill and perseverance to keep your vehicle moving in the right direction and avoiding sliding off the crest and becoming hopelessly bogged in a ditch. Chains, laboriously wrapped round the tyres before starting, were de rigueur in the wet season, and many people would take one or more of their servants with them to help push them out if they got stuck. A daily commute of that distance on such roads, therefore, was not to be undertaken lightly, and I am sure that this was a factor in my parents' eventual decision to move down to Nairobi.

Ma, too, looked for employment and at one time had a job going around to the dairy farms, of which there were many in the area, collecting samples from which butter-fat content was assessed. She often used to take me with her, Tony being left at home with the ayah. It was fun driving out to the farms, with the rich fruity smell of cow manure and mud, the clatter of the galvanised buckets, and the warm, delicious aroma of milk fresh from the cow, foaming as it was tipped from the buckets into the metal churns in which it travelled to market. Mechanical milking was starting to take hold, but there were plenty of dairies where it was still done by hand, and the milker would settle on his stool, rub vaseline on the teats, and then start the milk flowing into the bucket in strong rhythmic spurts. I would often be rewarded for my patience with a glass of milk, warm, unpasteurised, full of fat and cholesterol – absolutely delicious! It was returning from one of these visits that I fell out of the car. Cars did not even have seatbelts in those days, let alone the elaborate paraphernalia of child restraints, capsules, and child-proof locks without which any responsible parent nowadays would not contemplate travelling. Mucking around in the back seat while my mother (fortunately quite slowly and carefully) negotiated the narrow farm road, I chanced to lean on the handle of the door which swung open suddenly, depositing me on the roadside. My departure had been so abrupt that I had not even time to cry out, and my mother, oblivious of my absence, drove on for a mile or so until, wondering at the silence from the back, she turned to look, and there I wasn't. The slow speed of the car and the long grass growing beside the road ensured that no real harm was done, but it was a shock for us both.

People in the early 1950s were not as obsessed as they are now about the vital importance of providing formal education for toddlers as soon as (or even before!) they are out of nappies. Nonetheless, this side of my development could not be ignored indefinitely.

The local primary school catering for the needs of European families in the area (for education was still racially segregated in those days) was at Tigoni, some eight to ten miles away. Transport was therefore a problem, with only one car, which Pa needed to go to work in Nairobi, and no public transport to speak of. Consequently my first steps in education were taken through the medium of the Rift Valley Correspondence College. I knew about the Rift Valley – our friends, the Streatfeilds, had a farm in the Kedong Valley, an off-shoot of the great Rift, at the base of the escarpment – and I envisaged the College being somewhere near there, though it seemed a strangely inconvenient place to site a school. No doubt it was actually based in a dusty little upstairs office in Government Road in downtown Nairobi.

Anyhow, the lessons appeared regularly in the post, enclosed in rather coarse off-white envelopes with the College crest on, and my little writings, drawings, and sums were sent back for correction. The College presumably did a reasonably good job, for by the time I actually went to school, the year we left Limuru, I could write, do simple arithmetic, and was already an avid reader. This last characteristic I undoubtedly inherited from my mother, who had always read widely and well. I devoured the Enid Blyton books – Noddy, the Famous Five, the Secret Seven and so on – the Rev. Awdry's Railway Series, recently much back in favour with the resurrection of Thomas the Tank Engine, and, of course, that most magical of children's books, which I can still read with enormous enjoyment, Noel Langley's immortal "The Tale of the Land of Green Ginger". To give an idea of the sort of books I was reading at that age, I have a copy of Sir Percy Fitzpatrick's classic "Jock of the Bushveld" given to me on my 7th birthday, and I remember that I was given this because our old copy of the book, belonging to my Uncle Peter, had been severely damaged by the rain when I left it up in a tree house where I had been reading it. "Jock" was another great favourite, and I was captivated by the adventures of the brave bull-terrier and his master, together with Jim the Zulu who had fought at Isandhlwana and Rorke's Drift, Rocky the American mountain man, wise and taciturn, and all the other characters so faithfully drawn from Fitzpatrick's own experiences on the South African lowveld at the end of the nineteenth century. It was an interesting coincidence that later our firstborn, Tamsin, came into the world when we were living right in "Jock of the Bushveld" country, and the Komati River formed part of the background to her infancy, just as it had been a narrative thread in my own childhood.

Eventually, for social, if not academic, reasons, the Rift Valley Correspondence College had to give way to a real school, and, for the first term of 1952, I went to Tigoni Primary School. The transport problem was solved by enlisting the help of several families in the neighbourhood who also had school-age children. These included the Mortons, who had two sons about my age and the Gills, with the bossy Veronica, slightly older than I and infinitely wiser! If we came back with the Mortons, we would walk back from their home through a small patch of forest, where Veronica would chill our blood with the tales of the murderous men who were, perhaps, lurking behind these very trees, from where they might emerge at any moment with razor-sharp pangas and simis to cut us to pieces. Any suggestion that my father would protect us was dismissed scornfully by Veronica. "Don't be silly!" she cried. "They'll chop him up too!" Obviously she knew more than I did about the unrest in the country that was soon to flare into the Mau Mau Emergency.

Trips to Nairobi en famille were not frequent but always keenly looked forward to. Limuru had stores for the supply of groceries and hardware, but nothing that would tickle the fancy of a dedicated shopper. In Nairobi, hardware could be obtained from Gailey & Roberts, meat from Foster & Blowers, fancy goods from the Nairobi Emporium, Taws for chocolates, and just about anything from Woolworths, to say nothing of the little Indian shops down Bazaar Street selling spices, samozas, saris, gents' natty suiting, carpets, electrical goods, and a wide range of other exotic foods and clothing. We would have lunch at Torrs Hotel, just across from the famous New Stanley, outside which a stone statue of

Lord Delamere, a leading political figure in the early years of the Colony as well as a great pioneer in agriculture, gazed westward down the avenue which then bore his name (since renamed Kenyatta Avenue after independent Kenya's first President). A special treat during a trip to Nairobi would be a visit to the Coryndon Museum. This had a magnificent collection of stuffed animals and birds, as well as cases full of butterflies and other insects. Our favourite part of the museum was the gallery of illuminated displays of many of Kenya's most exciting animals. These were in darkened glass cases and when you switched on the light you were suddenly in the midst of the forest with an amazingly lifelike bongo or okapi or gorilla standing close enough to touch, if not for the glass panel between you. Our jolly Kikuyu ayah, Fat Maria, accompanied us on one of our visits. At the very first of these cases, the light was turned on to reveal, suddenly, a large leopard, snarling viciously as he surveyed the veldt from the mouth of his rocky cave. Maria gave a piercing scream and ran for the exit. She needed a lot of convincing that the animal was not alive, and did not completely relax until we were out in the sunlight once more. The only live exhibits at the Museum in those days were kept in an enclosure outside. These were huge tortoises, well over a metre long, and said to be hundreds of years old. They would lie baking in the sun, their wrinkled, scaly necks protruding absurdly from their battered and patterned carapaces, while they regarded us with unblinking and world-weary eyes.

Once a year, if we were lucky, though actually, I think, less often than that, we would go for a holiday to the coast. This was a considerable undertaking as Nairobi was separated from the sea by over 300 miles of very poor road. However, we usually made the journey by train, a journey that was in many ways the best part of the holiday. The train would leave Nairobi Station at around 5.00 p.m. in the evening, amid all the bustle of getting your baggage aboard, last drinks in the station bar, having your bedding delivered to your cabin, and then the roar of steam, the whistle shrieking, the staccato chugging of the engine, and then the more measured beat as the wheels got purchase on the rails and slowly started to pull the long train out of the station. The locomotives were the giant Beyer-Garratt engines, widely used in Africa, which were articulated, with a wedge-shaped water tank in front of the normal circular boiler. We would travel First Class, in 4-person compartments linked by a connecting corridor. The two top bunk beds folded away for convenience during the day-time, and you had your own little wash-basin under the window, with a wooden lid so that it could double as a card table. The window had, so to speak, three layers, each pulled up with a sash – a wooden shutter to close it off altogether, a gauze mosquito screen, and a glass panel which let in the light but not the air. We were discouraged from sticking our heads out of the window because of the possibility of getting smuts from the engine in our eyes. Dinner would be announced by a steward walking down the corridor banging a melodious gong. Ravenously hungry, we would hurry along to the dining car, where we would eat an excellent meal served at our tables on heavy china plates emblazoned with the crest of the East African Railways and Harbours (EAR & H) while the Athi Plains hastened by outside in the gathering dusk.

Despite being an "Express", the train made frequent stops at all sorts of little stations, to pick up passengers or goods and to fill up with water. Early in the night, vendors would come to the window of the carriage to sell roasted mealies (mahindi) or other goodies, and you could stretch your legs on the platform in the soft warmth of the African night. Later, of course, we slept, but sometimes in the night you would wake and peer out through the window at some little bush station, with cheerful voices chattering in Kiswahili and men sleeping wrapped in blankets on the platform. Sultan Hamud, Konza, Mtito Andei, Tsavo – the names had a magic about them. Tsavo in particular recalled the famous man-eaters of Tsavo, a number of lions that terrorised the area during the construction of the railway at the end of the nineteenth century until they were shot by Colonel Patterson. The railways still kept, as a museum piece, the coach into which one of the lions had forced his way to carry off an unfortunate British engineer. These days were long gone, however: there were still plenty of lions and other game about, but man-eaters were mercifully rare.

One of the most magical things about the rail journey was waking up the next morning in a different world. Having boarded the train in the cool arid highlands, you would awake to a new dawn in every way. The air was warm and moist, the smells were rich and exciting, as the train made its way the last few miles to the coast through groves of banana trees and coconut palms. By the time the gong summoned us to breakfast, we might already have had a glimpse of the sea and could scent its tangy presence on the horizon. As the train pulled in to Mombasa station you knew for sure you were on holiday. In the early years we usually went from there to Malindi, a resort some 60 miles of the usual bad road north of Mombasa. To get there we had to cross two creeks which, in those days, were traversed by ferry. The earliest ferries were human-powered, hauled across the river by pulling on two chains which ran from either bank and through brackets on both sides of the ferry. The ferry gang would walk in a continuous line on each side of the ferry, hauling the chain as they went. As they did so, they sang a sort of sea-shanty-cum-calypso in Kiswahili, into which would be woven information that the foreman had elicited from the ferry's passengers ("The bwana and memsahib and bwana kidogos have come from Limuru –hola, hola – going to Malindi to stay at Lawford's – hola, hola" and so on). Eventually, of course, the singing ferries were replaced by more prosaic ones powered by a diesel tug-boat, and a lot of the magic was lost. Nor was that the only disadvantage of the change: I remember arriving to use the Kilifi ferry once to find that the tug-boat motor had died mid-stream, and the ferry, fully laden with people, vehicles and livestock, had drifted well upstream (fortunately the tide was coming in). There was nothing to be done but wait patiently until the crew had got the engine going again. Actually boarding the ferries always struck me as a rather hazardous process. Buses, cars, and trucks would edge down the steep concrete ramp towards the ferry, whose own ramps had been lowered onto the shore. It seemed to me that there was every chance that the ferry would be pushed away from the bank by the vehicle's front wheels, causing it to drive straight down into the water. An alternative scenario for disaster saw the car or truck driving right over the wooden blocks at the other end of the ferry and sinking like a stone in the warm salty water beyond. As far as I know this never happened, but the authorities obviously shared my apprehension to some extent, since all passengers were obliged to dismount while their vehicle was boarding or leaving the ferry. Getting off was almost as exciting as getting on, with each vehicle having to take the steep ramp at a run and not stop until it reached the flatter road at the top while the passengers ran cheering up the slope behind it. On the way to Malindi we passed, and sometimes detoured to see, the abandoned old Arab city of Gedi, ruins overgrown by bushes and creepers, a relic, presumably, of the period of Arab settlement along the East African coast. The Arab influence along the coast was still very strong, and the language, Kiswahili, contains many Arabic words. Although Kiswahili is spoken all over East Africa, including Ruanda and parts of the Congo, it was only spoken properly by people along the coast and in Tanganyika. The language reached its lowest form on the lips of urban Europeans, where it was known as "Kitchen Swahili" or "Kisettla".

Malindi in those days was a much more modest resort than the international package tour destination that exists today. There were four hotels – Lawfords, The Blue Marlin, The Sindbad and the Eden Roc, and a number of simple cottages for rent. These typically had concrete floors, roofs thatched with makuti (coconut palm leaves) and large open apertures in place of windows. Crime was not a problem then, and the climate was so warm and humid that you needed no protection from the wind, which blew in refreshingly from the ocean. At Malindi, as elsewhere on the coast, there was a coral reef a few hundred yards offshore, so swimming was completely free of the menace of sharks. The only shark attacks on the Kenya coast occurred in the harbour at Mombasa where there was a substantial break in the reef through which the ocean-going ships could pass. The East African coast is very tidal, and low tide would leave vast expanses of flats exposed. I can remember in the very early 50s seeing a small plane land on the sand at Malindi at low tide. In many places it was possible to walk out to the reef when the tide was out, and we could also hire one of the local fishermen to take us out to fish or goggle on the reef in his *ngalawa,* a dugout canoe with outriggers and a small sail. When the tide was high, the surf could be quite exciting, and we used to body-surf lying down on short curved wooden boards which could give you an exhilarating run for 50 to 100 yards through the foaming shallows before grounding on the sand.

Holidays at the coast were idyllic, whatever age you were. The minimum of clothing was necessary – bathers or shorts or the ubiquitous kikoi, a sort of African sarong worn round the waist and for women, the khanga, a similar sort of garment to the kikoi, but longer and worn knotted above the breasts rather than around the waist (not, I might add, that Ma or any of my female relatives would have thought of wearing a khanga – much too raunchy, not to say suggestive of having "gone native"). The food was different too – lots of fish, often bought fresh from vendors who would come round to your cottage, and delicious fruit, such as paw-paws, pineapples, mangoes and several types of bananas, including the little, sweet, yellow ones called "ladies fingers".

The beach at Diani

There were new animals to see, several species of birds and butterflies that we did not get in Nairobi, and the huge brown millipedes, often 6-8 inches long, which used to leave their sinuous trails in the sand around the walls of the bandas and litter the ground with their discarded exo-skeletons.It was, of course, very hot in the sun, and we smeared ourselves with a rather pleasant-smelling golden jelly called Rayfilta, as well as taking vitamin pills that were supposed to deal with the disagreeable symptoms of sunburn. No-one had ever heard of skin cancer! Another problem at the coast was malaria, and we took prophylactic pills such as Paludrine or Daraprim and slept under mosquito nets, which we never bothered with at home. Swimming, surfing, sand-castle making and long walks along the deserted white sands of the beach made for lazy contented days. After our first couple of holidays at Malindi, we tended to go south of Mombasa to Jadini or Diani which were not quite so far, and even more beautiful. It was at Diani one day that I can remember saying to my parents "Oh! Look at Tony!" My brother, then aged about 18 months or so, was lying face down in the shallows, his head covered by an enormous straw hat. He was hurriedly rescued, fortunately without serious damage, but this incident left him with a deep-rooted aversion to water that he did not overcome for many years.

One local social event that was always enjoyable was the Limuru races. Pa had ever been a keen racegoer, and his field-glasses case bore tickets from countless English race meetings attended when on leave from India. It was no surprise that he soon immersed himself in the Kenya racing scene, and he later became the official Jockey Club Handicapper. There were three main racecourses in Kenya; at Nairobi, Nakuru, and Limuru, although meetings were also held from time to time in country centres such as Molo and Eldoret. The Limuru course, actually at Tigoni a few miles the Nairobi side of Limuru, was, and perhaps still is, one of the most beautiful little racecourses in the world. A lush green undulating oval surrounded by groves of darker green wattle trees, it doubled as a golf course, and the fairways crossed back and forth through the wooden barriers of the racecourse. In a hollow in the centre of the course was a cricket pitch containing what was, for many years, the only grass wicket in Kenya. Every-where else, cricket was played on matting, a sisal or coconut mat laid on a concrete or murram base. Race meetings at Limuru usu-ally had both flat races and steeplechases (some of the railings were movable to route the horses round the jumps when it was a flat race) and they were always colourful and enjoyable affairs. The buildings – stables, stands, weighing room, offices, bookies stalls etc – were mostly made of rustic poles and it gave the place a home-made and friendly feel. The last race at every Limuru meeting was traditionally the Kwaheri Handicap (*Kwa heri* being Kiswahili for "goodbye") at which punters could bid for a horse, the successful bidder becoming the horse's "owner" for the race. The bid money would then be pooled and divided among the three place-getters. Obviously, the better the horse, the more you would have to bid to get it and therefore the less you would stand to win. We always enjoyed the excitement of the auction, though as a boy I didn't understand it, thinking that the horses were actually being sold. It seemed odd to me that so many owners would happen to want to sell their horses at one time, and even more that one could buy such a big and wonderful thing as a racehorse, even a very bad one, for just a few hundred shillings.

Much has been written about the Mau Mau, ranging from Robert Ruark's sensationalised "Something of Value" to Elspeth Huxley's more realistic and empathetic "A thing to love", with numerous other tomes, scholarly and fictional, in between. Revisionist critics of the colonial era have sought to depict this episode, which lasted officially from 1952 until 1958, as a glorious nationalist revolt which eventually drove the British oppressors out of Kenya. There is a grain of truth in this, and certainly many of the nationalist leaders such as Jomo Kenyatta, the first President of an independent Kenya, saw the rebellion as one tool in their struggle for political rights. However, it must be remembered that it was confined to just one of the many tribal groupings in Kenya, the Kikuyu and their associated tribes the Embu and Meru. This meant that the majority of the African population of Kenya was not involved at all, and indeed a large minority of the Kikuyu people were not especially sympathetic. One of the reasons for this was the use of the old tribal customs (often horribly distorted) that the Mau Mau resorted to in an attempt to bind their followers to the movement. Quite a large number of the Kikuyu had become Christians, and rejected these atavistic oathing ceremonies as inconsistent with their new faith. Sadly, there were countless African martyrs made by the terrorists when they refused to bow to the old gods, and it is a fact that many times more Africans than Europeans and Asians died at the hands of the so-called freedom fighters. The other point to be made is that, militarily, the battle was lost by the Mau Mau. Although the Emergency was not officially ended until 1958, the power of the gangs had been broken by late 1956, and after that time the only fighters still at large were small groups of desperate men, living like animals in the forest, cut off from supplies and encouragement, gradually being hunted down by the increasingly confident and effective security forces. The first Lancaster House conference which initiated the process of Kenya's transition to independence in 1963 (or "sold us down the river", if you were a conservative settler!) only took place in 1960, some two years after the Emergency had officially ended. Nonetheless, there is little doubt that the Mau Mau Emergency provided further encouragement to a Britain that was increasingly weary, not to say financially incapable, of bearing an imperialist burden, and was keen to pass that burden on as soon as was decently possible to the peoples of her former colonies. As British Prime Minister, Harold Macmillan, was famously to tell the South African parliament in 1961, a wind of change was blowing through Africa.

All this was in the future, though. In 1952, a rising tide of attacks on isolated farmhouses and murders of government-appointed chiefs, missionaries, and Christian Kikuyu, brought matters to a head and the newly-appointed Governor, Sir Evelyn Baring, declared a State of Emergency. Jomo Kenyatta and others, seen as the brains behind the movement, were taken into custody and subsequently tried and jailed for their part in managing the rebellion.

For most Europeans, the Emergency came as a most unpleasant and inconvenient shock. One of the worst aspects of it was that a large number of their servants, including many in positions of authority and trust, were Kikuyu. Of all the East African tribes, the Kikuyu had shown themselves best fitted to adapt to the colonists' ways. An intelligent and industrious people, they had embraced the white man's culture, including his language and technical peculiarities, and had thrived. Their relative lack of warlike capability compared to some of their neighbours such as the Masai, a failing which had been a significant and crippling drawback in the days before the 'red strangers' arrived, was no longer a problem now that enforcers of Pax Britannica discouraged the use of spears as a means of settling land disputes. Moreover, much of the best farming land developed by the Europeans, including the famous White Highlands, was either on or adjacent to the traditional Kikuyu tribal lands. It was not surprising, therefore, that the Kikuyu should seek work on the farms and in the homes of the newcomers, nor that they should learn so much of the western way of doing things, and begin to develop, in many cases, a deep dissatisfaction with the limited role and opportunities which society as it was then constituted afforded them.

The Declaration of the State of Emergency, and the identification of the Kikuyu as potentially the enemy, meant that servants, often of many years faithful service, could no longer be trusted. Some Europeans divested themselves of all Kikuyu employees. For many this was quite impractical. They relied upon their Kikuyu workers too much. However, the trust was gone. The servants themselves were in an invidious position. Most of them were not political and had little sympathy with the Mau Mau. Many had worked for the same employers for years and developed genuine affection and loyalty for them and their families. But they knew that if they were awakened one night by a gang of their fellow-tribesmen with pangas in their hands and death in their hearts they would have little alternative but to go along with the terrorists' demands. We certainly employed almost all Kikuyu people while we lived at Limuru, which is in the heart of Kikuyuland, but after we moved down to Nairobi in 1952 our servants were invariably of other tribes, notably of the Abaluhya people from Western Kenya towards Lake Victoria. I have no doubt that our move down the hill to suburban Nairobi was largely in response to the dangers of the Emergency as well as making commuting to work easier for Pa and enabling a more satisfactory solution to the problem of our schooling. After I had spent just one term at Tigoni Primary, our lives were uprooted and we moved some 25 miles and 1,500 feet down to Spring Valley, a mere ten minutes' drive over mostly quite reasonable roads from the centre of Nairobi.

Chapter 2

Moving down the hill

The most significant change for Tony and me resulting from our move to Nairobi was educational. After just one term at Tigoni, with its two class-rooms, mixed years, and 'Jungle Gym' for sports, I was moved to the much larger, more organised and structured institution of Westlands Primary School ("The school colours are green" said my mother "the same as Uncle Peter's regiment", a remark that was doubtless intended to make me feel well-disposed to my new prison). Tony started his educational career at the Greengates Kindergarten, run by Mrs Penny, just around the corner from the primary school. Principal of Westlands when I started there was the redoubtable Mrs Angus, whose son John was also at the school, a little older than me. My memories of Westlands include playing marbles ('nyabs') in the dust at playtime, having free milk each morning (small glass bottles with the cream on top) and marching onto the sports field while the gramophone played 'English Country Garden'. I remember being told the facts of life one lunchtime by an older boy. Subsequent experience proved that his account was substantially accurate, but at the time I simply did not believe it: the idea that people would voluntarily do that sort of thing to each other with their bodies was just ludicrous and completely incredible. A rather odd boy called McGregor, with flaxen hair and an outlandish north-country accent who lived next door to the school, invited me to accompany him through the hedge to his home where, he said, there was lots of grub (he pronounced it "groob"). I had not the faintest idea what "groob" was, but it did not sound like the sort of thing my mother would have wanted me to be associated with, so I politely declined.

As far as classwork was concerned, my precocious reading, and what turned out to be a flair for maths, got me close to the top of the class, though I was never able to outdo the two best girls, Gillian Humphreys and Suzanne Burden. My handwriting, however, was and, alas, remains dreadful, and the copybook in which I laboriously scratched with the steel nib dipped into the inkwell set in the desk never saw any stars. I cannot remember doing any organised sport at Westlands, although I was keenly interested in games and intensely competitive from an early age (I remember getting immense satisfaction from winning the three-legged race and the egg-and-spoon race at a party I went to once, a feat that earned me one of those little guns that fire bits of raw potato). At the same party I saw my first magician, a turbaned maestro whose standard incantation was "Abracadabra! Simsullabim! I've got an uncle and his name is Jim!". I once asked my father if he thought I would ever play for England and was secretly bitterly disappointed by his careless, if perfectly realistic, reply "probably not". We certainly kicked a football around during our breaktimes at school, and Pa introduced us to the rudiments of cricket, but it wasn't until I went to school at Pembroke House that my competitive urges became focussed.

Moving from Limuru to the city may have reduced the direct threat from the Mau Mau but it did not completely remove its influence. I had become much more aware of the Mau Mau than I had been in the initial stages of the Emergency when my parents managed to shield us from much knowledge of the realities of the situation. One source of information, oddly enough, was the English newspapers. Tony and I would be taken down regularly to have our hair cut, either at the salubrious establishment of Theo Schouten near the New Stanley Hotel in Nairobi or a less grand Indian hairdresser in the Westlands shopping centre. While we were waiting to have our unruly locks reduced to a military 'short back and sides' and pasted to our scalps with liberal anointments of Bay Rum, we would read the magazines in the waiting room, of which our favourites were the Omnibus editions of the Daily Mirror and the Daily Sketch. From these I learned of such atrocities as the Lari massacre when an entire village, men, women and children, near Limuru were slaughtered by the Mau Mau. The incident that had the greatest impact on me was the murder of the Ruck family. The Rucks lived on a farm in the Rift Valley and were called to their back door by one of their servants late at night on the pretext of some emergency. Like the other millions of readers of the Daily Sketch I read in horror a lurid description of how their small son, about the same age as I was, watched from an upstairs window as the gang set upon his parents and hacked them to death, then lay quaking and helpless in his bed until the gangsters came up the stairs and chopped him to pieces where he lay. On one or two occasions in the early days, my parents would go out in the evenings, leaving us in the care of the servants. I can remember lying in bed, sweating and paralysed with terror as I listened to our servants chatting and laughing with their friends in the kitchen, just knowing that I was hearing a gang enjoying some light-hearted badinage as they sharpened their pangas for the slaughter, and that any minute now they would come for me. I got not a minute's sleep. After that, my parents would always take us with them when they went out at night, particularly after an incident which happened further up Spring Valley from where we lived when two young European boys wandering through the bush were unlucky enough to stumble upon a gang hideout and were murdered.

Many Europeans, especially in country areas, carried hand-guns with them, on their person or in the glove pocket of their car, and in many suburban areas, the residents organised them-selves into a sort of Home Guard which would patrol at nights. All Africans (indeed all Kenya residents ultimately) had to have an identity card or kipande (I still have mine) which they had to carry with them, and there was a strict curfew.

Pa being in the KPR was closer to the centre of operations than most people. On one occasion he had gone out to Thika, a small town in the coffee country some 30 miles North-East of Nairobi. Ten minutes after he left the police station there to return to Nai-robi, word came in that a gang had been spotted in a thicket near the railway between Thika and Nairobi. A strike-force of soldiers and police was swiftly put together and set out to deal with the terrorists. The resultant contact was a shambles from the point of view of the security forces. Two African police askaris were killed, as was a young British officer in the Black Watch, the only son of the distinguished war-time General, Lord Wavell. A senior police officer and one of my father's good friends, Peter Dean, was severely wounded, and died later in hospital. It was a sobering thought that, had the message about the gang come a quarter of an hour earlier, Pa might well have been involved. For years afterwards, whenever we went to Thika, which we quite often did to visit my half-sister, Rosemary, and her husband, Jacob, on the coffee-farm that he managed, we would point out to each other the little wood in the curve of the railway line about a kilometre down from the crossing where the battle had taken place.

After we moved to Nairobi I became a keen Wolf Cub and was occasionally allowed to ride my bicycle back from meetings, which were held at the school, a distance of probably about 3 miles. One wet and murky evening as I made my way home I reached the bottom of the long hill on Marlborough Road which I would walk up to get to Spring Valley Road at the top. The road was lined with tall gum trees, and the few houses were set well back. As I began to wheel my bike up the hill, already a little chilly and wet under my mackintosh, my blood suddenly ran cold. Half-way up the hill, standing under one of the gum trees, was a tall dark figure. In his hand, hanging by his side, he held what appeared to be and, as I drew nearer, could unmistakably see was in fact a panga, the long machete-like implement that the Mau Mau used with such horrific effect to chop up people and hamstring livestock. I stopped and considered the situation. I could go to one of the houses nearby but what would I say? There was very little traffic on the road, but even if I were to flag down a passing motorist, what then? I could ask for a lift, but what would become of my bike? In the end I could see no reasonable alternative to carrying on. With the drizzling rain moistening my terror-parched lips, and the thumping of my heart loud in my ears, I slowly pushed my bike up the hill towards the menacing figure. As I drew near I croaked out a greeting "Jambo!". "Jambo, bwana" came the courteous reply as I passed. On I walked, my ears straining for the sound of the quick dash forward to bring the razor-sharp blade down on my unprotected back. When I plucked up the courage to glance behind me, he was still standing there, the rain dripping off the rim of his battered felt hat, somebody's 'shamba-boy' making his way home with his panga, a versatile and ubiquitous agricultural implement long before it became an instrument of death and mayhem.

Chapter 3

Life in the Valley

The contrast between our old and our new home was considerable. From a 25 acre block of orchard and forest, surrounded by farmland and jungle, we moved to a 1½ acre rectangular suburban lot, surrounded on both sides by similar developed properties. From the old weatherboard and iron house at Mapsedge, we moved to a neat stone bungalow with concrete floors, a tiled roof and a well-kept gravel drive leading up to the front door. There was a separate guest cottage in the grounds which we used to let out. The garden was well-developed, with frangipani, bougainvillea, and other shrubs, and a number of fruit trees, including loquats and two magnificent avocado pears. It grieves me now to think that, because nobody in the family apart from Pa cared for avocados, virtually the entire crop would fall to rot on the ground or be used by Tony and me for target practice with our airguns (avocados made a satisfactory target in that you could dissect them afterwards and trace the path of the pellet as it penetrated the flesh and lodged in the harder core). There was a separate garage-cum-storage shed and my parents built on a spare room next to the house. The usual servants' quarters were screened by trees and bushes at the rear of the property. The boundary on all sides was marked by a dense kai-apple hedge which, with its thick, tough foliage and stems, and its long sharp prickles, made a very effective barrier. We had houses on either side, the road in front, and an area of undeveloped bushland behind, covered in liana bushes and low trees, an ideal place for hunting and stalking games. While we had nothing like the space we had enjoyed at Limuru, there was still plenty of room for our elaborate battles and range wars, motor rallies and bicycle races. There were also, of course, plenty of other children our age living nearby, and we would get together on our bikes and roam the neighbourhood, looking for trouble. Right at the end of Spring Valley Road lived the road's (and perhaps Nairobi's) oldest European inhabitants, the Elkingtons. Mrs Elkington was in her nineties and she lived with her daughter, Margaret, whom she called "Kiddie", a not entirely appropriate manner of address for a woman of seventy! They lived in a rambling wooden bungalow up on stilts that must have been built in the very early twentieth century – there was a photograph on their wall of a meet of the Nairobi Hunt in front of the house in 1905. They had a pack of dachshunds to which they were devoted and which would come pouring down the steps in a yapping throng to greet you whenever you visited the old ladies. The little dogs were grossly over-indulged, with the result that they became immensely fat: the older dogs in the pack could hardly move as there was very little clearance between their abdomens and the ground. After her mother's death, Margaret lived on in the house for a good many years. She had been a keen horsewoman in her youth, and though her shape, which tended rather to mirror that of her canine pets, by now precluded riding, she kept stables with a number of horses in residence, her own and those belonging to other people. Pa used to go up the road quite regularly to exercise one of her horses, a large bay colt called "Hermes".

One of the effects of the move to our new home was to substantially reduce the number of our retainers. Tony and I, at five and seven respectively, no longer needed an ayah, and the smaller size of the house and the garden meant that eventually we were able to get by with just one shamba-boy and a cook-houseboy. The culinary skills of the cooks employed by families such as ours varied enormously, depending as much as anything on the talents (both as cooks and as teachers) of the various women they had worked for. Our *Mpishi* (cook) from Limuru, who subsequently worked for my Uncle Peter, was a highly-skilled performer, whose chocolate eclairs were widely acclaimed. I do not recall any of his successors attaining his standard. After we moved to Nairobi, my parents did not employ Kikuyus again, and most, if not all, those who worked for us, as mentioned before, were Abaluhya. The two I remember best were Joseph who was our cook/houseboy for many years, on and off, and Masika (also called Lasto) who began as the shamba-boy at Spring Valley Road, but was subsequently promoted to inside duties, and was Pa's loyal servant and friend for the last years of his life. Joseph was a large cheerful man with a round face and a fine moustache. He was a Christian, and therefore only had one wife. He was much involved in the Salvation Army, and looked extremely smart, with his maroon and white peaked cap above his smiling black face. Eventually he left our employ to be a full-time Salvation Army Officer, though we stayed in touch, and he did occasionally work for us again on a temporary basis when the soul-saving was a bit slow. Lasto was a shy, quiet, and gentle person. I cannot remember anything about his family, and suspect that, like many rural dwellers who found work in the towns, he left them to look after his *shamba* in his home village.

Joseph in uniform

The move to the city gave Ma the opportunity to get involved in a greater variety of activities. For a while, she worked in the radio room of the Nairobi City police squad cars. However, Girl Guides remained her first love, and she worked as a trainer, an administrator, and finally as Colony Commissioner. During the holidays when we were still quite small, we used to have to go with her to Girl Guide Headquarters in a long weatherboard building near the Arboretum where we would play outside while Ma did her business. We were not permitted into the Arboretum which was apparently full of what my parents termed "bad hats", as well as, not surprisingly, a magnificent variety of native and exotic trees and shrubs. On the same property as the Girl Guide HQ was an arts and crafts centre which housed, among other things, Nairobi's puppet theatre. Of their productions I can only recall marionette versions of operas (we saw "Hansel and Gretel" and "Lucia di Lammermoor"). I suppose this was not unreasonable, given the absence of real live opera from the Nairobi cultural scene at that time.

Although a lot smaller than our Limuru property, Spring Valley Road provided more than enough room to accommodate the fantasies of small boys. Many of these were centred on war, and we used to have the most elaborate battles between the opposing forces of Animaland (the Good Guys) and the Germans (the Bad Guys) in which our toys, including our soft animals, were enlisted to take leading roles. It should be remembered that World War II had ended less than a decade before, and the conflicts of that struggle still dominated many of the books and comics that we read. Cowboys were also popular, partly inspired by the adventures of Jeff Arnold and his bewhiskered sidekick, Luke, as portrayed in the pages of Eagle magazine. One of my early passions, though, was cars, and I was fascinated by them, both real ones and models. We had dozens of Dinky Toys (if only we hadn't thrown them away, they'd be worth a fortune now!). The first tenant that I remember in our guest-house at Spring Valley Road was a pleasant young man called David Markham. He stayed there for some time, both before and after his marriage to a lady called Lesley, and his first child, Piers, was born while they were there. He was a motor-sport fanatic and I can remember watching a film of the great Jaguar victories at Le Mans in the early 50s in his sitting room. He was, more importantly, a participant in the early years of what became Kenya's greatest international sporting event, the Safari!

The early fifties were certainly memorable for me. 1952 is the first year I can recall being aware of as a year, and it seemed to go on forever. Apart from our move down from Limuru and the Declaration of the Emergency, we had the visit of Princess Elizabeth and Prince Philip. I stood outside the Police Station in Government Road where Pa was on duty, waving my little Union Jack as her cavalcade went by. The Royal Party was enjoying the unique experience of a night in Treetops, the hotel built in a tree overlooking a waterhole in the foothills of the Aberdare mountains, when the news came of the death of her father, King George VI, and her accession to the throne. Next year, of course, came the Coronation and we, like all parts of the loyal Commonwealth, were bombarded with picture books, medallions, mugs and other unmemorable memorabilia, mostly mercifully long since consigned to the tip.

Television had not yet reached Kenya, but we shared the great day by radio via the rather crackly medium of the BBC World Service. The BBC world news was rebroadcast each evening by the Kenya Broadcasting Corporation, and we got quite a few other British programmes through the Forces Broadcasting Station, set up to cater for the numerous British troops stationed in the Colony during the years of the Emergency.

I listened avidly to "Dan Dare, pilot of the future" as he and his offsiders, Digby, Hank, Pierre, and the magnificently named Jocelyn Peabody battled to save the universe from the forces of the evil Venusian Mekon, a small green man with an enormous head and a vestigial body who travelled around sitting on a sort of miniature flying saucer. Dan Dare also featured in print, in the pages of the magazine "Eagle", of which my parents approved because it contained some serious articles and historical comic strips. We even subscribed to it for a while, and there would be great excitement when the circular package arrived from the publisher in Britain, several weeks after publication. On the other hand, if I wished (which I did) to enjoy the exploits of Desperate Dan, Dennis the Menace, or Ali Baba and the Forty Thieves (led by the evil Mustapha Phagg – their trail was always marked by a line of forty-one smouldering fag-ends) as portrayed in the garish pages of Beano or Dandy, I had to rely on my friends.

It must be hard for today's young people to imagine growing up in a world without television. I'd like to be able to say that we made our own entertainment by gathering round the piano for a sing-song each evening, but alas nobody in my family played the piano (or, indeed, any other musical instrument). It is one of the few significant regrets that I have about my upbringing that my parents never thought to make us have music lessons. This was not because they did not enjoy and appreciate music, but just that it was not seen by them as an important part of a boy's education. At Mapsedge we had a clockwork gramophone which had to be wound up by hand after almost every record and used steel needles that came in a small packet and had to be changed frequently. My favourite record when small was called "Ting-al-ing-aling" ("The bells of love go ting-aling-aling for you but not for me" etc) with "Moonlight Bay" on the other side. We also had Frank Sinatra (to whom I had not yet developed an extreme aversion) singing White Christmas, and Doris Day singing the hits from "Calamity Jane". The records themselves were extremely fragile, being made of a hard, brittle, plastic, and I still recall my bitter tears when the first record I ever personally owned (Harry Secombe's melodious Welsh tenor telling the listener that 'We'll keep a welcome in the hillsides') was accidentally dropped and smashed to smithereens.

There was tremendous excitement a few years after we moved to Spring Valley when Pa splashed out and bought a record-player, an amazing device, powered by electricity, whose needle never needed replacing, and could not only play the new-fangled long-playing records, but could automatically play a stack of them, one after the other. Was there any limit to human ingenuity?

We had not been long at Spring Valley when a new family member entered our circle. Rosemary, Pa's daughter from his first marriage and some 20 years our senior, came out from England for a holiday. Part of that holiday was spent at Malindi on the coast, and here, by the swimming pool of the Eden Roc Hotel, she met Jacob Prebensen, a tall, handsome Norwegian, with lean Scandinavian features and a sardonic twinkle in his blue eyes. As so often happened at Malindi in those days, the result was life-changing. They were married in the little stone church of St Mark's, Parklands some months later, the reception being at our house, where Tony and I enjoyed our first wedding. After the honeymoon, they returned to the coffee farm that Jacob managed near Ruiru, and not too many years after that Tony and I were uncles, with two little girls, Elizabeth Anne and Wenche, to hold our hands with adoration and make us feel most pleasantly mature! Our half-sister Rosemary was a most lovely person, with a quiet and good-humoured strength of character that ideally complemented Jacob's nervous energy and helped counter-balance the wide streak of Nordic pessimism within him that too often turned, as he grew older, towards depression. My parents liked and respected Jacob, though they continued for many years to pronounce his name Jake-ob in the English manner, rather than Yar-kub in the Norwegian. A Sunday afternoon drive out to the coffee farm for tea with Rosemary and Jacob was always a treat, Rose relaxed and motherly, Jacob trim and precise in starched khaki shirt and shorts, with the little girls later on to be hero-worshipped by, and a succession of Alsatian dogs all called, for some reason, Zipp.

Rosemary with Wenche & Elizabeth

Good uncles!

One of the advantages of working for the Government which Pa, as an officer in the KPR, did, was that you qualified for 'long leave' in Britain, at the generous rate of 6 months every 7 years. This provision no doubt originated in the days when the work of shouldering the white man's burden was a good deal more dis-agreeable than it had become by the 50s, and when travel back to the mother country took much longer than it now did after the advent of air travel. At all events, by 1954, the Durrant family had qualified for a rejuvenating transfusion of British civilisa-tion, and we rented out the house, left cats, dogs, and servants in the care of the tenants, and boarded a BOAC DC4 Argonaut for the thrill of a journey many thousands of miles north to what the Africans termed Ulaya, we children in the playground called Pongo, but what most adult Kenya Europeans (even those who had never been there) simply called Home.

Six months in a foreign country – the cold, the pollution; learning to live with elderly relatives; Battersea Funfair, Hamley's toyshop in Regent Street, the Farnborough Air Show, Madame Tussaud's and the Tower of London were memories to cherish.

With the coming of autumn, it was time for us, like migrating birds, to fly south again, and once more we climbed aboard the Argonaut for the long journey (Rome, Benghazi, Khartoum, Entebbe, Nairobi). Entebbe was always an interesting place to land for those of a nervous disposition, because you approached the airport over Lake Victoria. It was hard to tell, peering through the porthole, how high above the water you were, until the upturned faces of fishermen in their dugout canoes made you realise that you were not very high at all. As the engines throttled back and the flaps drooped, it seemed as though the pilot was about to give us cause to try out the life-rafts, when suddenly the green lake-shore loomed underneath and we sank onto the comforting black runway on which we bounced before resuming our normal relationship with the earth. The approach to Nairobi was also quite exciting as we came in over the Athi plains, yellow and parched in desperate need of the short rains expected any day. Mount Kenya was, as usual, swathed in cloud, but the unmistakable humps of the Ngong Hills to the West brought a lump of recognition to the throat. As we got lower, herds of wildebeeste, zebra, and various types of antelope, would gallop away from the sound and shadow of the plane and before long we were walking down the portable staircase into the bright, dazzling light and heard again the familiar sound of Kiswahili. We were home.

Six months is a long time in the life of a nine-year-old, and it was tremendously exciting to revisit our old haunts, and greet the people and animals we had left behind. The servants were well and greeted us with broad smiles and warm handclasps. The dogs were also in fine fettle and ecstatic at our return, and Mittens, the Siamese cat, welcomed us with the haughty disdain of her kind. Unfortunately, "Buggins" the tabby, and "Pinkle-purr", my black cat, had disappeared. In Pinkle's case I suspect he had found himself another billet where the standard of service, or the rate of absenteeism, was more to his taste, for, though he did return a few times after we had come back, he never stayed for long, and eventually disappeared for good. In his place we acquired a tortoiseshell kitten, found by Pa on one of his country trips, and christened "Josephine" because of her coat of many colours. Josephine was a rather neurotic little animal with a nervous disposition, who did not get on well with the other pets. Mittens, of course, despised her as an inferior creature, and the dogs' attitude, though they were, of course, quite used to having cats around, was more than a little ambivalent. The result was that poor Josephine developed a severe persecution complex, not without some justification. As the old joke has it "No, Mr Brown, you are not suffering from paranoia: they are out to get you!"

For me, the excitement of coming home was almost overshadowed by an even more thrilling change on the horizon. This was to be my last term at Westlands Primary. 1955 would see me begin a new challenge as a boarder at Pembroke House.

Chapter 4

Pembroke House

Pembroke House or PH, as it was affectionately known by generations of boys and staff, was a peculiarly British institution. Its very motto, "Anglus in Africa sto" (I stand, an Englishman in Africa) symbolised the attitude of the British colonial power, conjuring up, as it did, an image of a standard-bearer of civilisation, bravely holding his ground amid the swirling hordes of barbarians. Established in the late 1920s to prepare the young sons of empire-builders for entry into the English public school system, PH was (and, indeed, still is) sited in extensive grounds some three miles from the little town of Gilgil, on the floor of the Rift Valley about 75 miles north-west of Nairobi. Travellers by road from the city or the coast would turn up the road from Gilgil towards Thomson's Falls. Travellers by train would be met at the station and transported up the hill by the school bus. In either case, after a short journey you would turn into a gravel drive after passing under the railway line, and draw up in front of an impressive stone building which housed the dormitories and the Headmaster's quarters, as well as the staff room and sundry other offices. The class-rooms and other staff accommodation were tacked on to the main building and reached by covered walkways which provided some, though not complete, protection from the tropical rainstorms which occasionally beset us. In front of the main school building, encircled by the drive, was a lawn in the middle of which usually stood a slip-cradle, on which the more senior boys, whose privileges included being allowed to walk on this lawn, would practise their catching.

When I arrived in the Lent Term of 1955, Kenya was still in the grip of the Emergency, a fact that was apparent from several arrangements at the school. For one thing, the entire school was surrounded by a barbed wire fence, a structure that would have been about as useful as the Maginot Line, since there was no gate to prevent the gangsters walking up the drive. Many of the extensive bush areas within the school grounds had also been fenced off and were strictly out of bounds, which of course made them ideal for those addicted to the evils of tobacco and other nefarious activities. On the two front corners of the main house, crude stone pill-boxes had been constructed into which the askaris who guarded the school at night could retreat to fight off attackers. The alarm would be raised by means of one of those hand-operated air-raid sirens familiar to those who lived through, or saw films of, the London Blitz. As a last resort, there was a huge black rocket in a stand at the top of the stone steps at the side of the school. In the event of Mau Mau attack, this was to be ignited, sending a fiery message of alarm to the heavens and, more importantly, to the British army camp just down the road on the outskirts of Gilgil. Seeing the signal, the army would presumably leap into their trucks and come roaring up the road to rescue us. We boys had been told that, if the Mau Mau came, we were to dive under our beds (where the terrorists would presumably never think of looking) and remain there until the all clear was sounded. As it happened, I hadn't been at the school for more than a few weeks before our emergency drill was put to the test. Soon after we had retired one night there was a loud shout, a shot, a crash and a horrified shriek. As one we were over the side and under the bed, where we lay cowering on the floor next to the chamber-pots. It seemed an age that we lay there, quaking with terror, hardly daring to breathe, our ears pricked for further sounds of battle and for the crash of broken glass that would herald the forced entry of crazed gangsters, their *pangas* and *simis* already dripping with blood, and the whites of their eyes yellow with bhang and hate. In fact, it was probably little more than five minutes later that one of the masters came into the dormitory, turned on the light, and said that we could get back into bed, it was all a false alarm. What had happened, we learned the next day, was that a servant had been carrying dinner on a tray to one of the masters who lived in a house in the school grounds separate from the main buildings. An askari on patrol, suffering from over-indulgence in pombe, the home-brewed African beer, had seen this white-clad form before him, challenged it, and not getting a swift enough response, had opened fire with his trusty .303. Fortunately his aim was consistent with his state of sobriety, but his target, though unhurt, gave a howl of dismay, dropped the laden tray, and sped off into the night.

Flying planes from the staircase at the top of which the emergency signal rocket was kept

PH when I was there was quite a small school, with about 75 boys aged between 7 and 13 years. We were all boarders of course, and came from a wide range of backgrounds. Our parents were farmers and civil servants, professional people and businessmen and women, who shared one common aim for their sons which was to gain entry for them to a suitable British public school. Over the years PH had provided a steady stream of boys to such schools as Winchester, Radley, King's Canterbury, Sherborne and Shrewsbury. The academic goal was the Common Entrance examination, success in which was then (and perhaps still is) the 'open sesame' to the English public school system. Many, like me, did not in fact go on to secondary school overseas, but the syllabus was geared towards those that did, so that, for instance, we learned French and Latin from the beginning, which was not the case in Government primary schools like Westlands. There was considerable flexibility in the form structure, and essentially you were moved up when you were judged ready. I started in the 3rd form (for some reason there was no 1st form, and the 2nd form was very basic) but within my first term had been promoted to the 4th form, and progressed fairly rapidly from there through the 5th and 6th forms to the top class, the Special 6th, where I probably spent nearly half the 3 years and 2 terms that I was at PH. Not having done French or Latin before, I struggled to begin with in those subjects, but made up for that in English, Maths and History.

The teachers we had at PH were, to say the least, a very mixed bag. The Headmaster, Mr Christopher Hazard, whom we not very imaginatively called Quelch, after the Head in the Billy Bunter stories, was an extremely tall man with slightly hunched shoulders and a lined, leathery, and weather-beaten face like an ancient turtle. His neat tooth-brush moustache and his teeth were stained yellow by the cigarettes he constantly smoked. His wife, Mrs Hazard, was a tall, thin, kindly lady, who would occasionally invite homesick little boys into the Head-magisterial apartment where they would have their spirits revived with cups of cocoa and, if they were really lucky, marshmallows. There was quite a strong military element among the staff. Long-term teachers included

Col Pratley, a solid and florid man with a pipe, a comfortable wife, and a Golden Labrador dog, and Col Mallinson, an ex-India hand who knew my father. Col Mallinson was tall and thin and thus unkindly known to us as Maggot. His other nickname was Pombe, on account of his alleged fondness for the bottle. One of my classmates was a red-headed youth called Bodley-Scott (we almost always called each other by our surnames, occasionally nick-names, but hardly ever Christian names). Bodley-Scott, who had a very well-developed sense of humour, rigged up within his locker in the class-room a device which sent water dripping into a tin can at regular intervals, making a steady and very irritating "ping, ping, ping". After a while, the poor Colonel could stand it no longer and demanded to know what was making the noise. "It's the pombe-annoya bird, Sir" said Bodley-Scott seriously while the rest of the class stifled hysterical giggles. "It's very rare!" Maggot turned a deeper shade of purple and his moustache bristled, but there was nothing he could do. Some of the staff were more transient. There was one young man who had just finished his National Service during which he had been dropped as a para-trooper on the canal zone during the 1956 Suez crisis, and there was a naval ex-officer (so he claimed) called Purgavie, whom I hated as much as he disliked me.

One of the Maths teachers was called Rhombus by us because of his strangely-shaped head. He was a fiery fellow, and it was generally considered that he went too far when he clipped one of our classmates so hard round the ear that he temporarily deafened him. The boy, von Senger, nicknamed Rhino, had a terrible stutter, which had prevented him from getting out the answer quick enough to satisfy the teacher. It was the scale and unfairness of the thumping that offended us, not corporal punishment as such, which was used by most of the teachers occasionally in the class-room, and accepted by the students as part of the deal. The Headmaster himself taught French, and I can recall him bending one unfortunate lad over his knee and beating some of the French irregular verbs into him. Despite this he was a good French teacher, with a genuine love of the people and the language which he managed to pass on to at least some of those under his care. He had a somewhat ponderous and dry sense of humour, as when he would tell us, to illustrate the importance of the correct accents in French, that the sentence "Le peuple emu repondit" could mean either "The excited people replied" or "the purple emu laid another egg", depending on where you put the accents.

The music teacher was Mr Liddell, a nervous man with skull-like face and wire-rimmed glasses. His nick-name was Itchy, after his habit, in moments of stress, of plucking at his chest with both hands. He was particularly keen on proper enunciation. "No, boys!" he would cry, his hands plucking feverishly, "This hymn is Holy! Holy! Holy! not Howly! Howly! Howly!" I am afraid it has been Howly! Howly! Howly! to me ever since. One of the most influential teachers at the school as far as I was concerned, was Mr Leo Mackie, who taught History and Latin. An Australian by birth, he was quite shy and reserved, but when moved to anger, his face would contort in a 'grince' (his word – a sort of humourless leer) and he would say "You little maggot!" as his arm reached out to grab an ear and pin the offender to the desk for a brisk whack with the board ruler. His genuine interest in the subjects he taught again rubbed off, and I have retained a fascination with history in general, and ancient Rome in particular. He was very friendly with the Head, with whom he shared a passion for trout-fishing, and on their weekends off they would pack their gear into Mackie's ancient Landrover and set out for one of the several rivers running off the Aberdares that were stocked with rainbow trout.

Undoubtedly the outstanding teacher at PH when I was there was a young man called Brian Hanbury. Tall, clean-cut, with slightly unruly dark hair and incredibly expressive eyebrows, his dominant characteristic was his quite extraordinary energy. He walked everywhere at the double and would sweep down the corridor from his quarters to the Special 6th classroom where he taught us Maths in less time than it took Bodley-Scott to prime the "pombe-annoya bird" and shut his locker. Not that we ever tried such tricks on Hanbury. He would see straight through them. Why, he even had eyes in the back of his head! "Warren-Gash!" he would say, as he stood with his back to us writing the answer to an exercise up on the board in his impeccably neat handwriting," if you flick that lacky-band at McCauldin I shall give you cause to regret it!". Mischief nipped in the bud! That sort of thing impresses small boys no end! Whether it was sharing with us the sacred mysteries of Algebra, teaching us to shoot on the range with the school's .22 air rifles, or coaching the 1st XI soccer, Mr Hanbury brought an energy and enthusiasm to everything that could not fail to inspire us. He was a born teacher and Pembroke House was lucky to have him.

While the teachers were, in some respects, a motley crew, the same could be said of many of the boys. They came in all shapes and sizes and from many different backgrounds. There were hearty extroverts who appeared to have not a care in the world, and shy little lads who missed their mum and would weep bitterly into their pillow the first few nights of term and after each weekend exeat. We had our share of genuine eccentrics. Chris Seex was one such, a boy with straight black hair, spectacles and slightly prominent teeth. He anaesthetised rats and opened them up to see how they worked. He was said to have tried out the anaesthetic on his mother during the holidays and knocked her out for several minutes. It certainly worked well on the rats too. Dorman and Teasdale were an inseparable pair, Dorman large and a bit slow, Teasdale athletic and bright as a button. They spoke their own language and would rush around the school reciting meaningless rhymes in unison in a strange sing-song voice.

The only boys at the school I knew from before were our family friend George Streatfeild and a boy called Jeremy whom I had met on holiday at the coast the previous summer. Then, we had got on well, and I looked forward to renewing our friendship. Alas, at school it was a different matter, with Jeremy being a senior and me just a "new gink" (the 'g' is hard, as in 'gimlet'). Any friendly overtures on my part were met with haughty scorn, and in fact he was responsible for the first bit of active bullying I remember. I had made, as one did, an ant-lion maze on a piece of cardboard, with the walls of paper glued on and the resultant channels filled with sand through which, as we watched in fascination, the poor old antlion, or polly-wog as we called him, would burrow along backwards, presumably trying to find a way out. Jeremy found me with my maze which he proceeded to snatch from my hand and destroy, informing me that I wasn't allowed to make one as it was a privilege for senior boys. My reaction – "Jeremy! That wasn't a very nice thing to do!"- was gleefully reported by him to his mates and caused them much hilarity. The only other bullying I can recall from school days was being ragged for what I was told was my "la-di-da" speech. My parents despised the so-called "Kenya accent", with its clipped South African inflection and liberal use of the word 'man' (or rather 'm'n') and we had been strongly discouraged from adopting it. I can still remember the mortification of the first time I read the lesson at Sunday prayers at PH when my plummy and over-expressive rendering of the scriptures reduced the audience to helpless mirth and me, when I resumed my seat, to bitter tears. Useless for well-meaning friends to try and comfort me by saying that my detractors were only jealous because I had read it so well. I knew!

Alan Rudge, Nigel Hall, CD, Charles Dorman

The making of ant-lion mazes was just one of a constant succession of crazes that swept the school, some quite fleeting, others almost perennial. Marbles (nyabs) was a recurring favourite, skipping held sway one term, the aim being to see how long you could keep going without stopping (the record was several hundred skips). One term everyone was making the little tractors with a pencil stub, a cotton reel, a section of wax candle and an elastic band. The elastic bands also came in handy when the craze was for stringing several together to make a fly-shooter and see how many flies you could kill. The school grounds were infested with grass rats, which would rush along their well-defined runways through the grass before diving down their holes. The school would sell us rat-traps at 2 shillings each and paid a bounty of 10 cents per tail, so you only had to catch 20 rats to move into the profit zone. I set my trap once where the runway ended on a little rise above the hole so that the rat would rush along, leap down onto a sort of banking and virtually bounce off it into his hole which was at right angles to the run. When I hurried to check my trap at lunchtime, I found the trap sprung, the rat's head lying beside it, and a trail of blood leading down the hole whither the rest of the wretched animal had continued under its own momentum. This was very unfortunate for the rat, but not good news for me either, since the bounty was paid strictly on tails, not heads.

An enduring craze was the construction of 'shacks' (what an Australian child would call a cubby). Although some of the bush areas had been fenced off to save us from the Mau Mau, there was still plenty of room for construction, and most boys had a shack, usually shared with a number of friends. Some were little more than bush bivouacs, with crude stone walls and branches forming the roof. Others were extremely elaborate, dug into the ground, with several rooms connected by tunnels, and roofs made of scavenged building materials that were almost waterproof! Apart from the fun of building them, the result was a hideaway where you could retreat to chat, read or, in a few cases, smoke.

Another very significant craze during my time at PH was butterfly-collecting. Kenya has many of the world's most beautiful butterflies, from the huge colourful swallow-tailed Papilios, to the swift, powerful Charaxes, and the tiny Blues, also quite strong flyers, some with delicate tails at the edges of their brilliant blue wings. For a few boys, such as my friend Oliver Heathcote, collecting was a serious business, with the specimens being carefully set, mounted and labelled. For many, the thrill of the chase was the thing. The commonest prey was the African Monarch (*Danaus chrysippus*), a largish reddish-brown butterfly, which came in a number of variations, including a very handsome type with black tips to its front wings and, rarest of all, one with white patches on its back wings. Commonly, those left at school on a Sunday afternoon would take their nets down to the playing fields and prowl around until the cry went up "African Monarch!" and everyone would converge until a group of 15-20 boys could be seen running down the field, butterfly nets held above their heads, while the unfortunate object of their attention would bob along just out of reach until a downward swoop or a particularly high leap would bring him into range and he would be trapped in a net and brought to earth to the satisfaction of his captor and the envious admiration of the other hunters. Another common prey species was the Brimstone (White and Yellow) a fast-flying butterfly which passed over us as part of its migration route.

My "butty-hunting'" was at the more serious end of the spectrum, and over the years I accumulated quite an impressive collection, not all caught at school, but also at home, in the forests around Nairobi, at the Coast, and in other parts of Kenya where I went to stay with friends. I eventually donated my collection to the younger brother of one of my girlfriends.

Butterflies were not the only members of the insect kingdom to suffer from our depredations (the Green movement was very much a thing of the future!). Close examination of the ground, especially the grassed areas such as the playing-fields, would reveal a number of neat little holes, about 12-20 mm in diameter. These were the homes (and ambush places) of a species of large spider, which hid in the hole from which it could venture out to pounce on passing ants, grasshoppers, or beetles, dragging them down into its lair to be consumed. These spiders, which we called, quite erroneously, tarantulas, could be extracted from their dens by poking down the hole with a grass stalk. The spider would grasp the stalk in its jaws, and could be teased out of the hole, which was then closed off behind it with the swift insertion of a knife blade. I am sorry to say that we would then put the spiders in jars and make them fight each other, which they enthusiastically did to the death. I had a champion spider once, a huge black specimen, a sort of arachnoid Muhammad Ali, who defeated all comers with contemptuous ease. Unfortunately, while I was absent (batting in a House cricket match) my so-called friends set two other spiders onto Blackie. With fierce courage he fought them off and slew them both, but sustained wounds from which he died soon afterwards. I was devastated.

Like all schools of this type, Pembroke House attached great importance to games (i.e. sport). Cricket was played for about half of the year, and football (soccer) the other half. In the middle of the year, we had an athletics carnival, with high jump, long jump, 100 yards sprint, and hurdles. There was also a tennis court. Soon after I arrived, one of the staff introduced us to boxing and we trained enthusiastically. However, the subsequent tournament turned out to be such a blood-bath that the gloves were put away, never to be taken out again during my time there. There was also a brief attempt to introduce rugby, but it didn't catch on. Interestingly, in view of my later enthusiasm for the game, I had no interest in rugby at all and refused to even try it. A game where you could only pass backwards seemed ridiculous to me.

My budding love of games, however, which had little to feed on at Westlands Primary, reached full flower in the rich soil of PH. I was naturally quite athletic and intensely competitive, and this soon brought me success. In the athletics carnival in my first year I won all my events except the 100 yards, in which I was placed 2nd, and consequently won the Churchill Cup for the Junior Victor Ludorum. I never did as well again, though I still won the odd trophy. In cricket and football I also made my mark and was soon in the school's Under-11 team, and then, in the fullness of time, the 1st XI.

The school's playing fields were separated from the rest of the grounds by the Gilgil-Thompson's Falls railway line, and were reached by a footbridge. We were, naturally, strictly forbidden from going onto the railway reserve, although the frequency of trains was low and the chances of an accident therefore remote. This footbridge was the scene of what must have been one of the odder episodes in the history of the EAR & H. The railway, as I said, went to Thomson's Falls, which was the nearest station for the ranching area of Rumuruti. Here the Carr-Hartley family had their famous game farm, where they would keep wild animals that they had trapped for use in films and for sending to zoos overseas. Once during my second year at PH a train came by laden, among other cargo, with a number of animals from Carr-Hartley's, presumably en route for some exotic zoo. These included a giraffe, for which a special tall crate had been built, from the top of which its inhabitant peered with the customary expression of slightly supercilious calm in those liquid brown eyes that gazed out from beneath the impossibly long lashes. Unfortunately, the designers of the crate had not reckoned with the Pembroke House footbridge. The crate was a good foot too high to pass beneath it. The train was brought to a halt and stood there, hissing gently, while those in authority considered the problem. No doubt various alternative courses of action were explored – dismantling the top part of the crate and persuading the animal to bend his neck as they inched under the bridge, unloading the giraffe and transporting it round the bridge by road etc. In the end, the train was backed up, and a 50-metre section of track was taken up, the base dug out, and the track re-laid at a lower level, the whole process being reversed once the train had passed safely under the bridge. Naturally, this took several hours, and provided a fascinating spectacle for us curious schoolboys.

Sport was conducted in practice matches and then House matches before the School teams would be selected. There were three Houses, Coplestone's, Turner's and Pink's named, I suppose, after previous headmasters. I was in Coplestone's, called Copies for short, and our house colour was a sort of dun brown, not too dissimilar to the pale yellow of the House I was in at West-lands, which was Kent. (We were very patriotic at Westlands: the Houses were all named after royal dukes, the others being Gloucester (Red) and Edinburgh (Blue)). The school team played matches against other schools such as Nakuru Primary, Thomson's Falls, and Greensteds, a small school near Nakuru. Our great rivals, however, were Kenton College, a very similar school to ours, situated in Nairobi, and the Kenton games were the ones we most wanted to win. We also usually had matches against the Junior Colts sides of the two main European high schools in Nairobi, the Duke of York and the Prince of Wales. For our encounters with Thomson's Falls and Greensteds, schools even smaller in numbers than us, and therefore presumably correspondingly weaker, we usually fielded our Under-11 side. However, having travelled once with the Under-11s to Thomson's Falls where we were trounced 4-0, when the time came for the return match at home, it was decided to put up virtually our entire 1st XI, of which I was also by then a member. Mid-way through the game, the youngsters from Thomson's Falls, playing with extraordinary spirit, had held us scoreless, and I can still remember the scathing dressing-down that Mr Hanbury gave us at half-time, which left more than one player in tears. His words had their effect as far as the result was concerned, and we improved in the second half to win 2-0.

PH Football 1st XI 1957

Back row: G.Marston (& cat), C.Seex, J Forbes, J.Pembridge (capt) CD, T.Wilkinson

Front row: I.Shields, G.Streatfeild, P.Brown, P.Gilfillan

Something unique about the PH sporting teams was the manner in which we would send the news of the result back to Gilgil from away matches. The Headmaster was a pigeon-fancier and we had quite a large flock of racing pigeons who would spend most of the day endlessly circling the loft built on a platform near the school. When we travelled away, the birds would be placed in a large wicker container, with holes in the side through which they would peer in that rather gormless and slightly indignant way that pigeons have, while they cooed and gurgled to themselves. Immediately after the match, the score would be written on a piece of paper and placed in a small canister tied to the leg of the strongest flyer, and the flock would be released to find their way back to Gilgil. They usually all made it, although occasionally one or two went missing, victims no doubt of one of the raptors that were very common in the region. Being a "pidgie-boy" was a sought-after privilege, because only they were allowed up onto the loft, to keep it swept, make sure the birds had clean food and water, and check that they were healthy. As a pidgie-boy you would get to know many of the pigeons by sight, and while it would be stretching a point to claim that they were fascinating animals, there was no doubt that they did have differing personalities, and would reward their handlers with what passes, in a pigeon, for displays of affection.

The other distinctive feature of PH teams when I first went there was our mode of transport. While other schools might make do with a commonplace coach or, for the less fortunate, a truck with a canvas awning, our school bus had the Spirit of Ecstasy spreading its wings from the radiator cap. In short, it was a Rolls Royce! Having started life as a Silver Ghost saloon in 1913, it had seen service as an ambulance during the Great War, in the course of which it had found its way out to East Africa. After the war, it was purchased by the founder of Pembroke House, who replaced the ambulance body with a high square box fitted with seats and windows, and for almost the next 30 years this magnificent piece of automotive history did uncomplaining service carrying generations of PH boys to and from the station, sports matches, Remembrance Day services and other significant events in the school calendar. The speed of travel could best be described as stately, and it was a little inclined to boil under pressure (aren't we all?) but, with its long silver bonnet, and immaculate cream mudguards, it was a unique and marvelous machine, what Flanders and Swann, as in their immortal song about London double-deckers, might have described as a 'transport of delight'. When it was eventually replaced by a more efficient but infinitely more prosaic Austin bus, after I had been at the school about a year, it was not to enjoy a quiet retirement in some museum. On the contrary: a local farmer and vintage car enthusiast, Colonel Courtney-Curtis, father of a good friend of mine, 'Cow-face' Curtis (I was 'Currant-face' to him), bought it, removed the bus body to leave a flat tray, and used it for some years to take bags of grain to market. He was probably the only farmer in Africa with a Rolls ute! Colonel Curtis subsequently restored the car to something approaching its original incarnation as an elegant saloon and I believe it is still going strong in its land of original manufacture.

Mr Hazard was himself an old car fan. Apart from the Rolls, which technically, of course, belonged to the school, he had a 1930s supercharged Bentley, a magnificent long-nosed beast in British Racing Green. Just across the river near the school (a mere stream, really, known to us as the Gilgil Trickle) was the old motor-racing circuit of Langa Langa. Its use had been discontinued the year before I went to PH as it was considered too dangerous. In fact, I went to the last meeting held there. We thrilled to the raucous drone of the little open-wheelers, the Cooper-JAPs and Cooper-Climaxes, the shattering roar as the motorbikes took off, led as always by Victor Preston on his Norton Manx, the intoxicating smell of high octane fuel and burning rubber. One of the last races that day featured two Jaguar XK 120s, the latest road-racing sensation from England. After several laps, one of the sleek open speedsters failed to appear with the other cars, and we learned later that it had gone off the road at the back of the circuit, killing the driver. I always assumed that it was this accident that rang the final knell for Langa Langa; motor racing in Kenya being subsequently transferred to a circuit near Lake Nakuru. Although no longer in use, the Langa Langa circuit remained in existence for some years, cracked and overgrown, but still recognisable, and Mr Hazard would occasionally take a select few passengers round it in the Bentley. As the acceleration built up along the back straight, and the grand old car's supercharger began to whine angrily, the wind would tear at your hair and bring tears to your eyes, and you would imagine yourself behind the wheel of a racing car, fighting to hold it straight as the stiffly-suspended wheels bucked and jerked on the uneven surface. As a strange post-script to the Langa Langa saga, many years later I went with my father for some reason to a sisal estate at Ol Donyo Sabuk, a place some 40 miles or so east of Nairobi. There, behind a shed on the estate, I found the shell of the Jaguar that had crashed that fateful day. I recognised it by its competition number, 119, still stencilled on the side.

Motor-racing at Langa Langa may no longer have been part of the entertainment at PH by the time I got there, but there were plenty of other things to do. One of the unexpected delights for me was riding. Pa was a keen horseman as a result, I imagine, of his polo and pig-sticking days in India, and it was naturally assumed that I too would learn to ride. I started my equestrian education at a couple of riding schools in the Nairobi area, the first at stables conveniently close to where we lived in Spring Valley, and then at another riding school across town. Neither establishment did anything to nurture my inherent sympathy with the horse. Both were run by the sort of tough, no-nonsense, women who often seem to be found around horses. The soft, feminine side of their nature, if it existed, which was very doubtful, was saved for their dealings with their four-footed friends. Certainly none of it was wasted on the clientele who, if they fell off, which I did, quite often, would be bidden sharply to stop snivelling and get back in the saddle if they knew what was good for them. It is not surprising that riding lessons were far from the highlights of my life. I am sure, too, that I was subconsciously influenced by the fact that the only person of around my age whom I knew personally who had died, a boy named John Bridger up at Limuru, had met his end by falling off a horse.

Riding at Pembroke, however, was quite different. The lady in charge, a farmer's wife called Mrs Scholes, was, it is true, a fairly solid horsy type cast in the usual mould, but she did have a good heart, and some sympathy for nervous little boys. She did not expect us to become Bengal Lancers overnight. The horses available for us to ride also provided enough variety in temperament to suit a range of capabilities. Real beginners for whom staying on at all was a significant challenge, could earn their spurs (which we were certainly not allowed to use – I speak figuratively) on two small fat ponies called "Silver" and "Chips". Their natural gait was a very slow amble which they would reluctantly increase, in response to frantic kicks in the flank and castigation with the little switch that we were allowed, to a slow trot. Encouraging them to a faster rate of progress than this was beyond the energies of most of their passengers. Their relatively sedentary life had given them a broad beam and a placid disposition, rendering them ideal mounts to restore bruised confidence. Once you became more adventurous, there were horses that would offer you a more exhilarating ride. There were other advantages to riding at PH. Having mastered the fundamentals, we would go hacking in the bush which was far more interesting than riding around an exercise yard. We always rode in the morning before breakfast, and the fresh, clean smells of the African dawn, the dew on the tall grass as it brushed your stirruped feet, the steam rising off the flanks of the ponies into the cool air, and the gentle cooing of the ring-neck doves in the trees, all cast a spell that made you feel it was good to be alive. The day's ride always finished with a gallop up the playing fields to the School at the top, where we would dismount and hand our horses over to the syces who would walk them back down the fields to the stables. This was much the best part of the whole ride: the horses, of course, knew quite well that this was the end of the working day for them, so they needed little encouragement, and even Silver and Chips would launch their tubby little frames into an enthusiastic imitation of the Charge of the Light Brigade. Thundering up the grassed playing areas, ducking under the soccer goalposts, vying to be the first to clatter over the railway crossing and into the yard near the African staff village where we would dismount, was a most exhilarating experience, and would send us into breakfast with flushed cheeks, bright eyes, and a feeling that all was well with the world.

The breakfast after riding was another bonus. Most normal school mornings, we had a plate of porridge to start the day, and this would usually be dished out well before we arrived at the breakfast table. The consequence of this was that by the time we got to eat it, the porridge had congealed into a cold lump that swivelled in the bowl like the workings of a hydraulically mounted compass – not very appetising! On riding mornings, though, we were fed separately from the common horde, and the porridge was dealt out hot and steaming while we watched – delicious! Food is something in which most small boys take a keen interest, and consequently the catering arrangements had a big impact on our life. Compared to the standard of fare provided in today's boarding schools, the food at PH in the 1950s was certainly inferior in taste and variety, though probably not in quantity. Hot and stodgy was the rule, with the fresh fruit and salads that are considered an essential part of the diet of today's youth being largely absent. The meat was always very well cooked, doubtless to ensure the destruction of any harmful parasites, and if this also destroyed any taste, well, too bad! The school had a small herd of donkeys, whose function was to pull a cart which was sent into Gilgil each day to collect the mail and groceries. The death of one of these animals was followed by the introduction onto the menu of a new form of meat (actually a sort of braised beef) which became immediately known as 'Dead donkey'. The desserts followed the same pattern, solidity winning out over delicacy. The commonest was steam pudding, either with currants ("Big Dough") or without ("Little Dough"). These would have been quite palatable (we were, after all, growing boys and therefore very hungry) were it not for the invariable addition of large dollops of custard and what the school chose to describe as 'cream' but what was in fact a peculiarly revolting sort of clotted skim milk. These supplements could lessen the appeal of even the most toothsome pudding. The other aspect of meals which today's schoolboys might find hard to cope with was that you were not allowed to leave anything. You did not rise from your place at the table until every morsel on your plate had been consumed or, if you were really desperate and ingenious, secreted somewhere about you to be furtively disposed of afterwards. This rule left its mark: even today, I always clean my plate to the last crumb, though nowadays, unlike then, I am usually able to arrange beforehand that the plate does not contain anything I really don't like.

Exeats, of which we were usually allowed three per term, afforded us, apart from a brief taste of freedom, the opportunity to vary our diet somewhat. If you shot or caught something edible on your exeat, you were allowed to take it to the kitchen on your return where it would be cooked and served up to you at dinner that evening. There was always a buzz of excitement when the servant from the kitchen entered the dining hall bearing a large tin tray on which would sit the well-cooked corpses of doves, pigeons, or trout, which would be delivered to the successful hunters under the envious gaze of their friends. One evening, there was a gasp of astonishment when the tray entered the room, followed by a roar of laughter. The Matron, Miss Farrant, (known as "Atom Bomb" because of her explosive temperament) who was on duty, went to see what the fuss was all about. When she caught sight of the tray, her face went puce and her eyes flashed dangerously behind her spectacles. In the middle of the tray lay a couple of dozen large locusts, deep fried, their legs and feelers a crispy brown. "Whose" she hissed menacingly, "are these?" A small boy called Wells tremulously raised his hand. "Out!" thundered the Atom Bomb, and Wells and the locusts were banished from the dining hall forthwith. Poor Wells was rather hard done by, I think. After all, locusts had featured on the menu of no less a personage than John the Baptist, and many of the Africans regarded them as something of a delicacy. I was never tempted to try them myself, unlike that other entomological dietary supplement, flying ants, which we used to pluck out of the air and pop straight into our mouths after removing the wings. (Taste report: quite bland and tasteless. We really only ate them out of bravado, though they are quite nutritious if you eat enough of them – ask any aardvark).

Of our three exeats per term only one was an "overnighter" and even for that we seldom if ever went back to Nairobi. If it was only a day away, we usually went to friends locally. Sometimes we spent the day at the McKenzies who had a farm not far from the school. Grace McKenzie was a friend of Ma's and occasionally taught art at the school. She was a large, rather nervous woman, with huge pendulous breasts that were the subject of much unkind ribaldry from us horrible little boys. The McKenzies had a small swimming pool carved into the hillside in the forest, fed by a ram from the river far below. We loved swimming in it, but our enthusiasm was not shared by the Matron, Miss Farrant, who saw the pool as a source of most of the colds and ear-infections suffered by the boys who week-ended at the McKenzies. When I gashed my foot quite badly, necessitating stitches and leaving scars still visible today, Atom Bomb felt thoroughly vindicated. "That McKenzies' swimming pool!" she cried, her glasses glinting dangerously, "It should be banned!" Fortunately, she did not get her way. Swimming in up-country Kenya was always a somewhat hazardous occupation because of the risk of bilharzia. This condition, also called schistosomiasis, is caused by a tiny parasite (schistosome) which enters your skin from the water and finds its way to various bodily organs, notably the liver, where it flourishes and saps your vitality. It is endemic in much of tropical and sub-tropical Africa and, until the dreadful AIDS epidemic of recent years, was probably the most widespread and significant medical problem in the continent. It can be successfully treated, unlike AIDS, but treatment is expensive and normally requires hospitalisation, which puts it out of the reach of most sufferers. Years later, I did contract bilharzia when we were working in Swaziland and had a comfortable though rather boring sojourn in the London Tropical Diseases Hospital as a result. I am not quite sure why the McKenzies' pool was not considered a bilharzia risk. Perhaps it was too high or cold. The critical factor in the existence of the disease is the presence of a particular type of water snail which acts as vector for the parasite at one stage in its life-cycle and, if the snail cannot exist, neither can bilharzia. Fast-flowing rivers were therefore generally reasonably safe because the snails could not live there without being swept away. One of the most charming public notices I ever saw was in Uganda at the head of the Murchison Falls. At this point the Nile, already quite a substantial river, flows over a stretch of rapids before being compressed through a rocky cleft barely twenty feet across and thundering in a foaming torrent down to the crocodile-infested shallows some hundreds of feet below. At the viewing-point for this astonishing natural phenomenon the Game Department had seen fit to erect a sign warning that "Visitors are advised not to bathe here because of the risk of bilharzia". It would be nice to think that this was evidence of a bureaucrat with a sense of humour, though I fear that it is more likely to have been an unthinking response to a directive from on high that such signs be put up wherever tourists were likely to approach the river!

On the long break when we were able to spend the night away from School, we would usually spend that night with Uncle Peter and Aunt Peggie who lived in a succession of houses near Nakuru only about 25 miles away. Their last House was at Bahati beyond Nakuru where Peter grew strawberries and carnations to supplement his pension once he had retired from the Kenya Police. Up in the side of the Rift Valley, the farm had a fine view back down towards Nakuru and the extinct volcano of Menengai that dominated the town. There was also a dam to swim in behind the house, and plenty of room to explore and hunt. Apart from a flirtation with catapults which, in our hands at least, posed no real threat to the local wild-life, Tony's and my career as hunters began when we were given air guns. Our first air guns were Dianas, appropriately named but far from lethal weapons. The muzzle of the gun had to be unscrewed to load it with a concave lead slug, and a lever pulled back to compress the air. They were very inaccurate though probably capable of killing a small bird provided the range was no more than about 20 feet. As very few of the small birds that we encountered were foolish enough to let us get that close, their mortality was extremely low. I remember shooting at a green pigeon in a tall tree above me and hearing the pellet strike it with a distinct 'whup'. The bird did not even fly away at first but just remained on its perch, cooing indignantly and craning its neck to try and find the source of the gentle blow to its chest. The click as I recocked the gun for a second shot alarmed it and it flew away, doubtless unaware of its good fortune. My effectiveness as a hunter increased dramatically when I bought another air gun from Paul Whetham, a friend at school, a little BSA which fired waisted lead pellets of the same calibre as the Diana (.177) but with far more force and accuracy. With such a weapon one could range the bush with greater expectation of bringing home something for the School cooks to roast for Sunday dinner.

I don't think Ma really approved of us shooting things, and there were strict rules as to the birds that we were allowed to aim at. Pigeons were OK, presumably on the grounds that they were obviously edible, but doves (such as the little iridescent Tambourine doves that would stay crouched on the ground until you got near and then whirr off with a frightening sound) were not. We never told Ma that the ring-neck 'pigeons' that we often shot were not pigeons at all, but doves! Green pigeons were definitely fair game, especially as they were excellent eating, but they were also very shy and tended to roost in the security of flocks high in the trees, so we hardly ever shot one. The one species we were definitely encouraged to shoot was the mousebird. This was a smallish brown-grey bird with a jaunty crest, a very long tail and a raucous chirring call. They went about in flocks of 10-20 and were extraordinarily destructive of fruit and vegetable crops. I remember Pa one day finding a flock noisily completing the demolition of his cabbages and rushing out in fury with his shot-gun to blast them to kingdom come, a very inefficient and expensive measure of control, which cannot have done the cabbages much good either. The last sort of bird on our 'licence to kill' was the fiscal shrike, or 'jackie' as we called him, a quite inoffensive little black and white bird whose only crime was his, to tender souls such as my mother, repulsive habit of impaling his prey (grasshoppers, beetles, and very small reptiles) on thorn bushes and barbed-wire fences. This sensible and economical method of preserving his food supply was his undoing as far as we were concerned and it pains me to think how many shrikes we blasted off the telephone wires where they would perch to survey the scene.

After a hard day's hunting, we would enjoy a hot bath, a delicious dinner served by a smiling servant in spotless white kanzu and green tarboosh, and then some games before bed – Beggar-my-neighbour, Snap, Happy Families, Cluedo, and the sensational new board game, Scrabble. It was always with a sinking feeling and a heavy heart that I used climb into the car for the short journey back to Gilgil. Fortunately, the feeling never lasted long, and the excitement of comparing notes with your friends and the whispered confidences after lights out in the dormitories soon eased you back into the routine. Not that we didn't look forward to the holidays: some boys constructed, on the first day of term, elaborate charts showing the number of hours until the end of term, and would cross them off religiously every day. Most of us would do this for the last couple of weeks of term.

The dormitories at PH had been separate rooms, some on the ground floor (which also housed the Head's quarters and the staff room) and mostly on the second floor. Before I got there, presumably for security reasons during the Emergency, the internal walls had all been cut down to about 3 feet or removed altogether, making one big open-plan sleeping area. We had little privacy: our clothes were kept in communal wardrobes and I suppose we must have had some sort of chest for our few personal belongings. Today's boarders (and their parents) would have found it all very primitive. Allocation to dormitories was fairly random – there certainly did not seem to be any system of seniority and you were just as likely to be next to a prefect as to one of your fellow plebs. You could usually expect to be given the same bed for the whole year. Once, in about my second year at the school, Atom Bomb was making her nightly inspection when she noticed that I was not in my bed. A search of the lavatories having failed to turn me up the alarm was raised and a thorough search was begun. In the course of this, someone noticed that a bed in one of the adjoining dormitories appeared to have more than the usual number of occupants and there I was found to be! It had been my bed the previous term, and it seems that I had got up in my sleep and gone off to what my subconscious still thought was my pit. Neither I nor the other occupant of the bed woke up, and I needed a good deal of convincing about the truth of the affair next morning.

I suppose nowadays, even with 10-year-old boys, such an episode would give rise to all sorts of lewd speculation, but these were innocent times! Sex, even when one got to the upper end of the school, was not a matter to which many of us gave any thought at all, and with very few exceptions I believe we were most frighteningly naïve. The Head, Mr Hazard, obviously saw it as part of his duty to try and fill, to some extent, this gap in our knowledge but despite (because of ?) years of marriage to Mrs Hazard was evidently by no means ideally qualified to do so. At least once during our final terms, we more senior boys would be called into the Head's study after supper where we would sit in pyjamas and dressing-gowns, sucking thoughtfully on cups of cocoa, while Quelch rambled on at great length and quite incomprehensibly about the birds and the bees. Eventually we would be sent off to bed, warm, sleepy and full of cocoa, but not one bit closer to understanding the mysteries of the human condition with which our waking hormones were about to bring us face to face.

At the beginning of 1957 my status at PH received a boost when Tony joined me, having also done his first years of primary education at Westlands Primary. I now became Durrant major (Durrant ma. for short) and he was Durrant minor (mi.). A third brother (very rare) would be known as minimus (min.). When handing out our joint letters from home from his study window each lunchtime the Head would announce "Durrant bros!" We were encouraged (if not obliged) to write home every Sunday, and the replies (usually from Ma) were always a highlight of our existence.

One of the deficiencies of PH in the view of the Head was the lack of a chapel. After all, what was the point of standing, as an Englishman, in Africa, if one could not do so with all the paraphernalia of the official religion of the English which in those days, before the dominance of television (which did not reach Kenya at all until the 1960s), was still the Church of England? To have one built would have been prohibitively costly for such a small school, and he decided that we would build it ourselves. So it was that generations of PH boys got up before breakfast in the cool and misty African dawn and mixed concrete, wheeled barrows, manipulated form-work, and plastered cement. The basic construction was poured concrete around a rammed earth core and the variability in the performance of the workforces gave the building immense character. The stained glass windows were also to be home-made, and lead frames were cast in a shed in the grounds known (after the master who set it up) as the Randallising Shed. The interstices were to be filled in by chips of coloured glass glued to the flat panes. This, and much else, was not completed until long after I left the school and, indeed, I don't think I ever saw the finished article. A rather nice idea was to request boys leaving to purchase a chair on the back of which was a small brass plaque with your name and years at the school. These were initially used in the dining hall but were to be transferred to the

Chapel in due course. I hope that somewhere in there today stands a chair on the back of which is inscribed 'C.C.T. Durrant 1955-58'.

Like most schools, Pembroke became more enjoyable the higher up the pecking order you progressed. I cannot recall any systematic bullying of younger boys (perhaps the school was too small for much of that) but there was certainly a structure of privilege that divided the sheep from the goats. I have mentioned that only senior boys were allowed on the lawn in front of the main building, and there was a short cut to the playing fields (that saved you all of 10 yards) which could be used only by prefects and those with Colours. Being good at sport earned one credibility more easily than anything else, and luckily I was good at sport and reasonably soon found myself in the 1st XI for both cricket and football (soccer). My athletic achievement never again reached the heights of my first year at the School but I did win the school tennis tournament in my final year. It was a strange coincidence that the losing finalist on that occasion, a country boy called Ian Shields, was the same opponent as in the only other tennis tournament I ever won, the Plateau Junior Championship played in Turbo in North-West Kenya in 1962. On both occasions I came from behind to beat a player who was fundamentally far superior to me.

I loved football and was a solid and reliable defender, being appointed Captain towards the end of my last season. As a cricketer, I was not truly very gifted but possessed a stubborn determination which partly made up for this. On one occasion I batted on with a large 'egg' on my forehead after heading a short ball in a match against Nakuru School. One of the Nakuru masters who was umpiring asked me if I boxed. I said I didn't. "Well, lad," he said prophetically, "you should!" His name was David Opie, and years later I played rugby with him at Nondescripts RFC. As I write this he looks down at me from the 1968 team photo. Some years after that he became headmaster of PH before dying tragically, accidentally drowned while fishing on a river in the Aberdare Mountains.

Standing Back Row :
J. Grieve, P. Brown, C. Durrant, R. Davies, C. Wright, K. McKenzie, A. Mann.
Sitting Middle Row :
T. Tory, C. Ball, A. Cole (Capt.), J. Ross-Munro (Pres.), A. Bryan (Vice Capt.), B. Granville-Ross, P. Plumbe.
Sitting Front Row :
W. Shawcross, J. Pritchard, M. R. W. Screen, D. Opie.
Inset :
G. Wright.

Nondescripts RFC 1968. David Opie seated in front at right

My strength in cricket was undoubtedly my fielding, and I would hurl myself around with great enthusiasm. It was for this that I was awarded my Colours, memorably on Guy Fawkes' night 1957. The PH cricket cap was all white (or rather, cream) with the School emblem, a Sussex martlet, in red on it. Before you got Colours, the martlet was sewn over so that the cap appeared merely white, and once you had been awarded them, Matron would unpick the thread to reveal the little red bird in all its glory. Our matches were against the usual schools but there were also a couple of games against adult opposition, a Fathers' Match and a match against the army, when there was a substantial British army presence in Gilgil. The adults on such occasions were handicapped by having to bat with "broomsticks" – bats the blades of which had been cut down so that they were only about 2 ½ inches wide. Despite this, the old men usually triumphed! Once a year, an official coach from the MCC in England would come out to Kenya to spread the gospel and ensure that we all played with a straight bat. His name was Mr "Watty" Watkins, and he used to spend several days at the school during which we would have a number of lessons. Not a hugely successful cricketer himself (I think he had played for Surrey 2nds) Watty was nonetheless an excellent coach and did much to imbue us with the correct techniques for batting, bowling, and fielding. A small and dapper man, he was always immaculately turned out in spotless 'creams' and smelled of aftershave and talcum powder. Although he must have found us very frustrating at times, he never raised his voice and his most powerful expletive was "Dear oh me!".

'Watty' Watkins 1956 with J.Pembridge, J.Sevastopulo
G.Marston & P.Whetham

I would not want to give the impression that school life at PH was dominated by sport, although that was certainly what I, as a boy, chiefly enjoyed. Academic standards, judged by our success in the Common Entrance examination, were high, surprisingly so considering the antecedents of some of the teachers, and bright students had every opportunity to extend themselves. Prizes, awarded at Speech Night at the end of the Michaelmas Term, during the time I was there were invariably in the form of books beautifully bound in navy-blue and red leather, embossed with the school emblem and motto. The first I received, in Michaelmas 1955, was for "Rapid Progress", an ambiguous accolade if ever I heard one!

Apart from sport and hobbies such as the collection of butterflies or stamps, and obeisance to the current 'craze', whatever that happened to be, we would occupy our times in the evenings reading or just chatting. Some people had crystal sets, a primitive form of radio receiver on which, if very lucky, you could direct the transmissions of the local radio station into your headphones. One or two people also had gramophones –my favourite song at this time being a jaunty little number left over from the recent war called "What does poor Pa do in the blackout?" (classic lines "He started on fretwork, he painted the bath, then Mother sat in it – we didn't half laugh!"). Reading material was also strongly biased towards the late conflict and we devoured "The Dam Busters", "Reach for the sky", "Boldness be my friend", "The white rabbit" and many more.

Although we did not have an organised music programme at the school (to my regret, I did not learn an instrument, and I cannot recall others doing so) we did have singing under the enthusiastic, if nervous, baton of "Itchy" Liddle. One of the highlights of my last year was the school production of Gilbert and Sullivan's "HMS Pinafore", a splendid affair under the direction and inspiration of Brian Hanbury. I played Captain Corcoran, an experience that I thoroughly enjoyed and one which stood me in good stead two years later when my next school decided to put on the same delightful piece of G & S nonsense.

HMS Pinafore 1958
Nigel Hall (Buttercup) & CD (Captain Corcoran)

Meanwhile, though, the halcyon days of extreme youth were drawing to an end and it was time for some serious decisions. As I have said, the vast majority of my fellows were destined for one of the English public schools. However, my parents explained to me that they could not afford to send me to both public school and university in England: if I wanted to go to Oxford, therefore, I would have to complete my secondary education in Kenya at one of the two main European secondary schools, the Prince of Wales or the Duke of York. This was a very easy decision for me. It was not that I particularly wanted to go to Oxford – university seemed an impossibly distant proposition that was not worth immediate concern. However, I had no wish to leave Kenya and travel to a country of which my experience had been that it was cold, dirty, and in many ways, very alien. It was also, if the papers were to be believed, inhabited by strange and evil creatures called "Teddy boys" and mobs of teenagers who screamed at rock and roll singers and ripped up the seats in theatres (behaviour to which, we little Colonial pre-pubes assured each other primly, we would never sink when we became teenagers!). My good friend George Streatfeild, who had left PH the previous year, had gone to the Duke of York and seemed happy enough. So it was that, in August 1958, at the fairly advanced age of 13 years, I left Pembroke House with its cosy family of 70 and enrolled for the last term of the year in the Duke of York School, Nairobi, then numbering, I suppose, more than 500 pupils.

Chapter 5

The Duke of York

The main school buildings: Chapel in the middle, Block 2 (Kirk & Mitchell houses) top right

The Duke of York School was founded in 1949 in response to demand from the increasing European population of Kenya, not all of whom could afford (nor, indeed, wished) to send their sons out of the country to complete their education. The other government secondary school at that time that catered for European boys, The Prince of Wales, was full and, rather than expand it further, it was decided to build a new one. The School was named after the Duke who had by then become King George VI, and a bell from the battleship Duke of York acted as our school bell. The school colours were maroon with an appropriately white York-ist rose, and the school motto "Nihil praeter optimum" (Nothing but the best) has always seemed to be entirely appropriate for an institution of that sort. The School's first Head of Classics, Tom Evans, who sadly died quite a while before I arrived there, wrote the school song "Suave Rosam", in Latin, which we were all required to sing on special occasions. The initial building pro-gramme did not keep pace with the enrolments, and when the first students were due to start at the beginning of 1949 there was nowhere for them to live. The Governor of the day, Sir James Mitchell, kindly offered the temporary use of Government House, so that it was in those august surroundings that the first Duko boys began their secondary school careers. The Governor's generosity ensured that one of the Houses was named after him, the others all being prominent European explorers and pioneers, Thomson, Delamere, Kirk, Lugard, Speke and Eliot. During my time at the school two other houses were opened, named James (after the first Headmaster) and Grogan, after Col Ewart Grogan, a Kenya pio-neer whose main claim to fame was having walked from the Cape to Cairo (the buses in his day being very unreliable).

Nearly all the students were boarders. There was one day-boy house (Eliot) but the 'day-bugs' were rather despised by the rest of the school. Living, as I did, less than 10 miles from the school it would have been easy for me to be a day-boy but my parents (or certainly Pa) took the view that boarding, and the toughness and independence of spirit which it presumably bred, were essen-tial elements of a British boy's education. Fortunately for me, I shared their views, though not necessarily for the same reasons. Boarders, it seemed to me, had much more fun, and the camaraderie and esprit de corps among the boarders was unique. I would have hated to be a day-boy, and the loss of freedom and lack of privacy that boarding inevitably entailed were prices well worth paying, as far as I was concerned.

The boarding houses were located in 'Blocks' of two houses, sharing a common dining room. In addition to the 6 senior boarding houses, there was a junior house into which boys went for their first year (or, in my case, first term). Here they slept in house dormitories under the supervision of two prefects from the senior house, whose promotion to that status was evidently intended to compensate them for the separation from their fellows. Our two prefects were Hendricks and Amos, the latter a brilliant trumpeter who was the star of the school dance band. Eddie Calvert ("The man with the golden trumpet") had had many tunes on the top of the Hit Parade in the late 1950s, and his numbers such as "Beyond Mombasa" and "Cherry pink" all featured in 'Minnie' Amos' repertoire. Prefects were usually, but not always, 6th formers. A boy who showed great leadership ability could be appointed a house or even a School Prefect in the 5th form and there were instances of 4th formers being School Prefects. One of the two Junior House School Prefects in my first year, John Henschy, was only in the 4th form (the other was 'Minnie' Amos who was a 6th former). There was a well-established system of "fagging" at the Duko similar to most English public schools, although the juniors (1st and 2nd formers) were known as "rabble" rather than "fags". Each prefect would be allocated two "rabbles" to be his personal servants. In the absence of his personal rabbles, a prefect could simply bellow "Rabble!" and any little boy within earshot had to come running, the last one there scoring the job. I was one of Hendricks' rabbles.

My duties included such things as making the prefect's bed, shining his shoes, pumping up the tyres on his bicycle, making him a cup of tea etc. It was not an onerous relationship, and not without its advantages. A run to the school tuckshop, for example, could often be rewarded by a share of the goodies you had been sent to buy. Hendricks was certainly a pleasant and easy-going master. When he left, I bought his bicycle from him, although it was a few years before I was able to ride it at school. This was a privilege reserved for prefects, and a very worthwhile one it was, with such a wide-spread campus, on which some of the sports grounds were a very long way away from the houses.

I realise that, in the modern world, the idea of small boys acting as servants to their seniors is repugnant, and the potential for abuse of the relationship was undoubtedly considerable. All I can say is that I did not personally experience anything that left a traumatic mark on me and cannot recall witnessing anything really dreadful. Certainly some prefects were less benevolent than others, but I do not remember anyone having his life made a misery. This is not, of course, to say it didn't happen: I was not an especially sensitive or perceptive child. The same goes for corporal punishment, which was certainly the order of the day throughout my school career. At Pembroke most of the masters administered the occasional ad hoc wallop with their hand or some other incidental instrument such as a black-board ruler. Official punishment was meted out by the Headmaster with the cane on a scale that depended on the severity of the crime, from 'one-on-each-hand' up to the maximum (short of expulsion) of "six-on-the-seat in front of the school" (never administered in my time at PH). The most I personally earned was four-on-the-seat, for the heinous crime, if memory serves me right, of breaking the Head's window with a cricket ball. At the Duko, punishment was significantly decentralised: although the Headmaster and the Housemasters could cane boys, in practice they very seldom did, and most punishment was inflicted with the tackie (gym shoe) by the School Prefect who was the Head of House. How painful this was depended to some extent on the muscular development and the state of mind of your Head of House and also (given that whackings were always administered after supper when you were in your pyjamas) whether a low blow struck a dangling testicle, which was, naturally, excruciating.

Apart from corporal punishment the prefects could impose scab duty and written impositions, which were usually essays on some particularly futile subject such "The noise grass makes when it is growing" or "A ping-pong ball, seen from the inside". The only exceptions were when one of the prefects decided to plumb the depths of his victim's lascivious mind and demanded two pages on "my perfect girl-friend".

The school was built about 5 miles from the centre of Nairobi on the Langata Road in what was then wooded countryside adjacent to the Kikuyu Reserve. A little further out was the suburb of Karen, named after the Danish writer Karen Blixen whose love affair with Denys Finch-Hatton was made famous by the film "Out of Africa". The Duko shared one feature with Pembroke House in that a railway ran through the school property, although in the case of the Duko it was the main Kenya – Uganda line, so there was a great deal more traffic. Needless to say, the railway was strictly out of bounds, as indeed was the African Reserve which lay beyond the fence to the North and West of the school grounds.

The Emergency was officially at an end by the time I arrived at the Duke of York, but in fact there was very little incentive to visit the Reserve unless you were a smoker. Devotees of this noxious habit would slip through the fence and make their way to the little *duka* (shop) where they could buy Crown Bird or, if they were really hard up and desperate, dreadful little cigarettes called Ten Centis. These were very thin, containing a vile black tobacco no doubt made from the sweepings of the curing-rooms. They were, however, extremely cheap. I was never a regular smoker although, like most boys, I tried it on a few occasions. If you were an addict, however, the extensive grounds with their large areas of thick bush gave you every opportunity of indulging yourself with little fear of detection. Another favourite smoke-hole was in the little shelters built out on the playing fields to act as pavilions for cricket. Perched in the roof of the shelter, you were invisible to anyone not standing actually under the shelter, and it was impossible to approach them unseen well in advance by the lookout peering through gaps in the *makuti* thatch, giving the miscreants plenty of time to dispose of the evidence if a master or prefect decided to investigate.

I was drafted into Delamere House, named after the Kenya settler leader whose statue then gazed thoughtfully westwards from its plinth outside the New Stanley Hotel. Our House colour was red and we were one of the four senior houses situated near to the main school buildings (Lugard and Speke were some way distant in the bush). The main school buildings – classrooms, offices, assembly hall, gym, and eventually chapel, were erected in a central area with an oval service road encircling it which we called 'Brooklands' after the famous British motor-racing circuit. The junior houses and Blocks I and II were adjacent to the service road, as was the Headmaster's home, the sanatorium, the squash court and the swimming pool. The houses had been put up in a hurry using a mud-core-within–cement-plaster construction and were only intended to be temporary structures to be replaced with something more substantial when time and funds permitted. Needless to say, they were never replaced. Each house had three dormitories running off a central corridor like the arms of the letter E, with an additional arm at the end containing the home-work room and senior studies. On the other side of the corridor were the ablution facilities, laundry store, and 4th and 5th Form common rooms. The more junior boys did their homework in the evening sitting at benches in the common work area. Prefects and at least some of the 6th Formers had studies (usually shared with one other boy) where they could work, brew up tea and toast, and pin up suitable pictures, though the censorship was quite severe: I remember one cartoon I had pinned up depicting a gravestone on which was inscribed "In loving memory of Sonia Jones who swerved to avoid a child and fell off the couch" being taken down by my Housemaster on the grounds that it was too raunchy! How times change!

The Housemaster of Delamere was a man called Dominic Spencer, a French teacher with beetling eyebrows who lived with his wife and three rather homely daughters in a house separate from but quite close to our quarters. His most memorable char-acteristic was that he had an artificial limb as a result of losing a leg to osteomyelitis in his youth, and consequently moved around with a lurching motion and a distinct squeak. This handicap of his was, as you may imagine, the butt of a great deal of unkind jesting which the poor man did nothing to deserve. I myself wrote a version of the famous Peter Sellers song, 'Grandpa's grave' about it ("They're removing Spencer's leg to make a drain-pipe; they're removing it regardless of expense; they will hack at his tin limb 'til it forms no part of him to satisfy the local residents – chorus: Oh! Oh! Oh! mate, don't amputate etc"). His wife Kate also taught in the school and both sang in the choir into which I too fairly soon enrolled.

The Head of Delamere in 1958 was also the Head of School that year, a boy named Mick O'Brian. A quite outstanding student, he was Captain of, and had Colours for, virtually every sport the school played, as well as being a high office bearer in cadets and a top performer academically. He seemed a god to me, and it was interesting to meet him again for the first time at a reunion more than 40 years later and discover that he was actually only a human being! Although nobody went to the Duke of York from Pembroke at exactly the same time as me, there were a couple I knew from previous years; neighbours from Spring Valley Road, several boys I remembered from Westlands Primary, and others, such as Hugh Aldous and Bryce Cowan whom I remembered from Thomson's Falls school, so it didn't take too long to settle in. The uniform was not very different to what I had grown used to at PH – normal wear was shorts with long socks and short-sleeved shirt (PH had a sort of safari jacket with huge pockets) but in grey instead of the Pembroke khaki. Ties were only worn with more formal uniform, which included the maroon blazer and either shorts or long trousers. Prefects were allowed to wear grey suits instead of the blazer and slacks. A jersey could be worn in colder weather. Nairobi, being near the equator but at an altitude of around 5,000 feet, had a very temperate climate - seldom desperately hot and never really cold, even during the rains – so the uniform was quite sensible. There was an official school hat, a slightly ludicrous trilby in grey with the maroon and silver band round it, but we were only required to wear this on relatively formal occasions, such as visits to town or to the Royal Show. No-one in those days had heard of skin cancer or, if they had, they didn't tell us.

Not surprisingly, as soon as I arrived at my new school I got stuck into the sport, representing the Junior Colts teams (Under 14 ½ years of age) in both cricket and football. It was very satisfying to go back and play against Pembroke House and (in the nicest possible way!) lord it over my old mates. There was also a keen house competition, and I remember the final of the Junior House Soccer competition, which we won, and having Hendricks and other great men wandering over to our half-time huddle and saying languidly "You chaps are absolute fanatics!" High praise indeed!

The Duke of York, like most schools then and many still, had three terms in its year. During the first everyone played hockey and many also swam, in second term everybody played rugby and a select few did athletics, and in the third we played cricket and football. Up to junior colts level, you played both football and cricket, but after that you had to choose one or the other. Because I had become by then quite a useful cricketer, I elected to play cricket when the time came to choose, but I always regretted not being able to play football, which I really enjoyed, and this was the main reason that, when I went on to university (in a climate where cricket and football did not share the same season) I returned to the football field.

In terms of academic progress, PH had served me well. I spent only my first term in the 2nd form and was then promoted with the rest of the class to the 3rd form. This meant that I was no longer a 'rabble', but it also meant that I was a year younger than most of my contemporaries. The Duko did teach Latin and French, and my time at Pembroke gave me a big advantage over many of my fellows who were unacquainted with these languages before coming to secondary school. The staff at the Duko were a very interesting lot with the usual mixture of genuine eccentrics, although they were almost all well qualified academically. The majority of the teachers were male, or at least nominally so. One teacher that I remember from my early days was a gentle and kindly man known to the boys as "Homo" Smythe. The admission, or open disclosure, of that sort of sexual orientation would have been enough to get him fired in those days, but I suppose the authorities chose to turn a blind eye. He once called the junior colts cricket team of which I was a part to his flat to show us how to put on box protectors! We dropped our drawers and fiddled with the complicated system of straps and buckles that were used in those days while poor old Homo sat in the background, giggling helplessly. He never actually laid a finger on us and we regarded him with a sort of affectionate contempt. The two most striking female members of staff were Mrs Ferguson, wife of Jock Ferguson, Housemaster of Thomson, and Mrs Skerman, wife of "Skunk" Skerman, Housemaster of Mitchell. One blond, one dark, both were good looking and exceptionally buxom, and consequently featured prominently in our lewd fantasies. One of the most interesting teachers was a lady called Vera Lewin, a slightly bowed middle-aged Irishwoman with cynical, humourous eyes twinkling behind horn-rimmed glasses, and a cigarette burning constantly at the end of a long holder. She drove to school in a huge green Chevrolet Impala, and was friendly with my parents with whom she often played bridge. Vera was an inspiring history teacher with a caustic tongue and a delight in revealing the frailties of historical figures that greatly endeared her to her pupils. She was also very easy to divert into reminiscences about her childhood in Ireland during the 'Troubles', or discussion of the lives and loves of the rich and famous. She once lost a bet with my friend Colin Wilcock about the size of Jayne Mansfield's waist: Colin claimed it was 18 inches, Vera didn't believe it, but she paid up happily enough when Colin brought in the relevant magazine article as evidence.

The other history teacher to have a big influence on me was Eddie Green, an old boy of the school who returned to teach there in 1960. Eddie was an excellent sportsman and I believe may have been Head of School in his time. He was quietly spoken with thinning fair hair and pale blue eyes and he had a great enthusiasm for history which communicated itself to us. He started a school historical society which used to meet in the evening and discuss historical events. We sometimes had guest speakers, the most memorable of whom for me was a man called Ian Henderson whom Eddie had known during the Emergency when he was doing his national service in the Kenya Regiment. Henderson was a farm-bred Kenya boy who joined the police at the outset of the Emergency. Unlike most Kenya Europeans, he spoke not only Kiswahili but also fluent Kikuyu, learned from the African lads who had been his playmates when he was growing up. This, and his intimate knowledge of, and sympathy with, the Kikuyu people, ideally suited him to be a pioneer of the "pseudo-gang" technique that was used with great effect in the latter stages of the Emergency. This method, first used by the British in Malaya, consisted of capturing terrorists, turning them around, and sending them back into the forest to operate against their erstwhile comrades. The pseudo-gangs were often accompanied by a European officer, naturally blacked up and heavily disguised. The courage required for this sort of thing was extreme: however effective the disguise, it was not likely to deceive a suspicious forest terrorist at close range and there must always have been the fear that, if their lives were under threat, the pseudo-gangsters might turn again and betray their white colleague. It never happened, though, and Henderson survived to receive a well-earned George Medal for his pains. His most famous operation was the search for and eventual capture of the most notorious of the Mau Mau forest leaders, described in his book "The hunt for Kimathi". When he came to talk to us, it was about a less well-known affair in which another noted Mau Mau leader, General China, had been captured, turned, and used in an (ultimately unsuccessful) attempt to entice more of the hard-core terrorists, including Dedan Kimathi, to give themselves up and come out of the forest.

By about 1956, the security forces' efforts to snuff out the Mau Mau by clamping down on their supply lines and detaining large numbers of their supporters had borne fruit, and the only terrorists at large were living like animals in the forests of Mount Kenya and the Aberdare mountains, hungry, desperate and dangerous, but no longer a significant political force. The Government's efforts to winkle out this residue took many forms – I remember at PH watching Lincoln bombers flying low over the school and hearing afterwards the distant crump of the bombs in the mountains. This tactic resulted in a lot of wounded and frightened elephants, buffalo, and rhino, which made life difficult for the security forces required to operate in the forest, but there is no evidence as far as I know that it had any effect on the Mau Mau. The pseudo-gangs were much more effective, and with the capture of Dedan Kimathi in 1957, the war in the forest was virtually over. Ian Henderson was a modest and quietly-spoken young man who was undoubtedly one of my boyhood heroes. He stayed on in the police in Kenya for a while after independence, before falling foul of some political pressure group and being deported. I did hear that he had gone down to Rhodesia, where he did good work in under-cover policing with the famous Selous Scouts, but I do not know whether this is true.

Another interesting innovation in my time at the Duko was the Political Society, brain-child of one of the English teachers, a dark-haired, sardonic man called John de Vere Allan. Kenya by 1960 had become a political cauldron. Despite the defeat of the Mau Mau, the British Government had made up its mind to divest itself of its African colonies as soon as could be decently arranged. The first to go was The Gold Coast, which became Ghana under the leadership of Kwame Nkrumah in 1957, and the writing was on the wall for Kenya. The Kenyan parliament, the Legislative Council, was initially entirely European, but during the 1950s there were first Asian members and then African nominated members. The Lancaster House Conference in early 1961 established a timetable for progress to full independence at the end of 1963, with universal suffrage and consequently a parliament dominated by Africans. The Political Society invited a number of politicians to the school to address us – old-time members like Michael Blundell and Wilfred Havelock, and the new breed of African leaders such as Mwai Kibaki, Tom Mboya, and Ronald Ngala. These were exciting times: the old assumptions were all being challenged, and the future was even more uncertain than it usually is.

Academically, the Duke of York, like most secondary schools in Kenya at the time, prepared its students for the Cambridge Overseas Examinations, the School Certificate, taken at the end of 4th form when you were about 16, roughly equivalent to the British 'O' Levels, and the Higher School Certificate, taken 2 years later and equivalent to 'A' levels. Most people would take about 8 subjects for School Certificate, and you would gain a Division I, II, or III pass, depending how many distinctions and credits you got. In your final two years your focus narrowed to possibly as few as 3 subjects, and you had to choose a general subject area – Arts (i.e. English, History, Languages etc), Maths, or Science. I was very good at Maths and competent at Biology, in which I got distinctions in the School Certificate, but my real strength lay in the Arts area, so for Higher School Certificate I studied History, French, and Latin, with English at subsidiary level.

However, all this lay ahead of me, with many hours of study to do in the meanwhile. The Science department had a number of interesting members of staff. Apart from the delectable Mrs Skerman, they had two one-eyed teachers in "Dogs" Davey and "Bungeye" Norman. Dogs (I have no idea how he got this nickname) was a laconic individual with a sarcastic sense of humour. "What must you do straightaway if you accidentally put your hand into a beaker of sulphuric acid?" Answers ranged from holding your hand under running water, preparing an alkaline solution to soak it in, running to the sanatorium etc. "No, lad," said Dogs, "the first thing you do is to take your hand out!" Laughter from the peasants, a faint sardonic gleam in Dogs' good eye. Bungeye (no puzzle about that nickname) was a keen hockey player and also the manager of the school dance band which, apart from playing at school dances and similar functions, used to do a stint in one of the hotels at Malindi on the coast during the summer holidays. Bungeye would doubtless position himself in the bar where he could ward off dehydration while keeping an eye (literally) on his charges as well as sizing up the local talent.

Mathematics was under the direction of Mr Kenneth Higson, a tall and elegant man with an exaggeratedly refined accent that used to come in for a good deal of ragging from us behind his back. He had a sharp wit though: a friend was walking downstairs one day, unaware that Kenneth was just behind him. Tripping and falling at the bottom, he let loose a 4-letter expletive beginning with 'F' which would hardly raise an eyebrow these days but back then was considered fairly fruity. "Nao, Thompson!" an icy cool voice came from over his shoulder, "the word is 'copulate' ". Geography and Latin were the preserve of Major Ian Reid MC, an immaculate and dapper man who was also the Officer Commanding the school's Cadet Unit. Most unfortunately for a person with such a surname, he had difficulty pronouncing his Rs, and was consequently known as Major Weed. "Wubbish, boy, Wubbish!" was a favourite reproof to a boy who had guessed wrong when asked to name the capital of Spain or decline the noun 'puer'.

He ran a very efficient Cadet Unit, though. Cadets was compulsory at the Duko for everyone over 14 ½ years of age. In addition to the army cadets, to which most of us belonged, there were navy and air force sections. There was also a band, consisting of bugles and drums. I spent less time in Cadets than most because of being a year younger than my peer group, but I enjoyed it and attained the rank of Sergeant before I finished. The head cadet my last year, a classmate called John Dunt, rose to be Admiral Sir John Dunt, 3rd Sea Lord or some such, so our training had benefits for some of us, at least. Training consisted largely of drill and weapons training, learning to dismantle, clean and (eventually) use the elderly .303 Lee-Enfield rifles with which the unit was equipped. The ones we had at school could not be fired as they had the firing pins removed, meaning that the only way you could kill anyone with one of them was to hit him over the head with it. We also learned the answer to such vital questions as "What is the weight of the pullthrough?" (Correct response: "The little piece of brass fixed on the end of it!") For some reason, I actually rather enjoyed drill – it must have appealed to some primitive instinct deep within me – and in particular loved marching to the sound of the band, especially on the rare occasions when we marched behind a full brass band. The school bugle band did have its limitations!

Once a year we would have a camp and would climb with our equipment into the back of trucks borrowed from the army to be transported to camp grounds behind the Ngong Hills which were only a few miles away or to some more distant destination. The only camp I went on saw us stationed near the British army depot at Nanyuki, north-east of Nairobi under Mount Kenya. Non-coms. from the British regiments stationed there at the time (the Coldstream Guards and the Inniskilling Fusiliers) were seconded to be our instructors and they drilled us endlessly, taught us again how to use our weapons, and escorted us to the ranges where we were able to actually fire not only the .303 but also the trusty Bren gun and the Sterling sub-machine gun with which the army was then equipped. We also saw being fired, although we were not allowed to touch them ourselves, the FN 7.62 mm self-loading rifle which had recently replaced the old .303 as the British army's standard infantry weapon. The camp had many of the benefits of living under canvas with few of the disadvantages. There were permanent ablution blocks, latrines, and kitchens, which took a lot of the inconvenience out of camp life. The food was very good, washed down by gallons of hot sweet tea, although this contained little white specks of undissolved powder that we believed to be a bromide added to the beverage to dampen our sexual impulses. I was particularly pleased about the relatively civilized latrines. It is in the Durrant tradition for this necessary function of life to occur in circumstances which permit a period of gentle meditation. I believe that the world is divided into those who have reading material in their loos and those who do not, and there is no prize for guessing into which category my family falls. On a previous camp in the Ngong Hills, a friend of mine, Tom Townley, had felt the call of nature in the middle of the night and stumbled off in the dark to the latrines, rough pits screened with hessian which were dug some 50 metres from the tents. Perched on the seat above the 'long-drop', doing what was needed, Tom heard the movement of earth from the pile behind the screen at his back, excavated to create the pit. Turning round he saw, silhouetted against the moon, an enormous lion peering curiously down at him. Unfortunately there was no independent verification, but it seems likely that the world record for the "drag-your-pants-up-and-50-metres-dash" would have been very comfortably broken!

The two high points of our camp were exercises out in the bush, the first a day exercise in the open veldt north-east of Nanyuki near Archer's Post in which we had to try and stalk the enemy in the middle of the woodland, and the second an overnighter on the slopes of Mount Kenya. For the latter we were transported by truck up to the furthest point accessible by vehicles and then had to walk up through the forest, camping for the night just below the line where forest gave way to heathland at about 12,000 feet. We did not carry tents and had to scrape our own bivouacs out of the hillside. Some went to enormous lengths to make a comfortable sleeping place, a sensible plan but one not without its pitfalls. Few of my friends had selected a reasonably flat area, for some strange reason relatively devoid of vegetation, and erected a most elaborate bivouac, using tree branches, ferns, and leaves to create some five-star accommodation. The Game Department scouts who had been sent along with us to make sure we didn't fall foul of anything fatally dangerous pointed out, with some amusement, that the reason this area was flat and bare was because it was part of a game trail, and there was every possibility of animals coming thundering along the path during the night. The tropical dusk was falling with its usual suddenness and it was not going to be possible to move the bivouac so there was nothing to be done but spray a cordon of urine around the area in the reasonable hope that this would deter any errant wildlife. I suspect, though, that it would not have been a restful night for the bivouac's occupants who would have lain awake for a long time straining to detect the faint trembling of the ground which would have heralded the approach of a rhino or a buffalo along the path. The wee barrier must have worked, though, for there were no nocturnal dramas.

The next day, rather stiff and cold in the grey dawn, for not a lot of light penetrated the forest canopy, we packed up and continued our walk up through the jungle until we emerged onto the moorland where the vegetation changed quite dramatically. The trees and bushes disappeared to be replaced by sedges and coarse grasses and the weird lobelias and giant groundsel. Just walking was hard work at that altitude, and some felt very sick. We climbed up to a rocky outcrop at about 15,000 feet called the Giant's Castle from which we had a grand view across the valley to the snow and ice-clad twin peaks of Nelion and Batian. Although, at about 17,500 feet, Mount Kenya is significantly lower than Kilimanjaro across the border in Tanzania which, at just over 19000 feet is Africa's highest mountain, it presents a far more formidable challenge to the climber. Kilimanjaro needs no special expertise and equipment, just stamina and determination: the final stages of the ascent of Mount Kenya are not for the novice. A few years after my modest excursion onto Mount Kenya, a couple of British soldiers achieved an extraordinary feat. Starting at the summit of Kilimanjaro, they ran down the mountain, drove in a Landrover to the main Nairobi-Mombasa road where they were picked up in a Jaguar XK 140 sports car and driven over 200 miles of dirt roads to Naro Moru, below Mount Kenya, at an average speed of 86 m.p.h. Here they were met by another Landrover which took them as far as it could through the forest and they then carried on up the mountain on foot, reaching the peak well under 24 hours after leaving Kilimanjaro. To stand on the summits of both mountains within the day was certainly a remarkable achievement. The fact, incidentally, that both mountains are not in Kenya today can be attributed to an aunt's generosity: apparently Queen Victoria wished to give Kilimanjaro to her nephew, Kaiser Wilhem, as a wedding present, and the boundaries of Kenya (British East Africa) and Tanganyika (German East Africa) were redrawn accordingly!

Climbing Kilimanjaro was something that many of us did towards the end of our school career, a sort of rite of passage. I did my climb at the end of 1960 together with about 5 other boys, a couple of them old enough to have driving licenses. We drove down to Arusha in Tanganyika (as it then still was) in a very elderly DKW van belonging to the amazingly trusting mother of one of us, Rob Burnup, drove up the foothills to an old hotel hidden in the tropical forest, and then walked. Even fit young fellows like us had a couple of porters to help us with our gear, as well as a guide to show us where to go. Many people had far more elaborate entourages. At the same time as we went up, there was an Indian Maharajah on the mountain. Evidently a man of means, he carried nothing himself, but was accompanied by about a dozen heavily laden porters to carry his substantial needs, as well as two guides and his personal batman. Personally unencumbered, he would stride off confidently every morning, leaving us languishing in his wake. He had his come-uppance though; on our way down from the final ascent, we passed his highness half-way up the scree, green to the gills with mountain sickness. His batman and the guide would lift him a few feet up the mountain and then drop him facedown to retch and recover before trying again.

The first two days saw us climbing steadily upwards, first through jungle and then moorland and heath. We spent the nights in simple but reasonably comfortable wooden cabins named, in those days, after various German dignitaries and explorers. Here we heated up tins of beans and ate the energy-rich food – sultanas, chocolate, and glucose tablets – that we hoped would get us to the summit. On the third day we eventually emerged onto the saddle, windswept and almost devoid of vegetation, that lay between the main peak, the sugarloaf of Kibo to the west, and the craggy spikes of Mawenzi to the east, made of a soft and treacherous rock that renders the climbing of it impossibly dangerous. Some years before, an East African Airways Dakota with about 15 people on board had crashed into Mawenzi, and its wreckage and occupants were still there, visible if you knew where to look. No-one had ever been able reach the crash site. With our back to this, we trudged wearily along the saddle to the top hut at about 15,000 feet. At the time we were there, the top huts were in the process of being replaced. The old ones had been mostly dismantled, and the new ones, although largely complete, had some significant deficiencies. The worst of these was that there was a three-inch gap between the walls and the floor, through which the icy wind would whistle. Keeping warm was an impossible challenge. Water boiled at such a low temperature at that altitude that you could not even enjoy a decent cup of tea! Ma had thoughtfully provided me with some lightweight thermal blankets, but even with these inside my sleeping bag and with every bit of clothing on, including three pairs of socks, boots, gloves, mittens and balaclava, I was so cold I could not sleep. We were roused well before sunrise at about 3.00 a.m. to begin the final climb to the summit up the scree. There are at least three reasons for starting this early, the first being that the pebbles of which the scree is made are more closely bound together in the icy night, making walking up it rather easier, though it was still a question of 'three steps up and one step back'. The second was psychological; too many would have given up had they been able to see the sheer slope they had to climb. By the time the sun had come up you could tell yourself you were almost half way there and might as well finish it. The third reason we did not appreciate until the sun actually did start to rise and we could look back and see the glorious red and yellow of the African dawn spreading across the sky behind the pitch black ragged crags of Mawenzi, gradually taking over from the black of the night as the stars faded before its advance. It is without doubt one of the most beautiful sights I have seen. Inspired by this we plodded slowly on, weak and nauseous but determined to make it, and eventually there we were at Gillman's Point, the 'tourist summit' where we could sign the visitors' book. The highest point on the mountain, Kaiser Wilhelm Spitz (now Uhuru Peak) required a further walk through the snow round the crater, and none of us felt obliged to do that, so we turned around and literally ran down the scree. It was amazing to take as little as 20 minutes to go down what had just taken us anything from 3 to 5 hours to climb up. Collecting our packs and equipment at the top hut, we carried on at a rollicking pace, spending just one more night on the mountain before returning to our vehicle, paying off the guide and porters with much hand-shaking and back-slapping, and then climbing into the old van for the journey back to Nairobi. Filling up with petrol in Arusha, we pooled our remaining resources and calculated that we should just about have enough for a round of soft drinks. Where else to go than the Safari Hotel, then Arusha's plushest hostelry, where, we recalled, were supposed to be staying the actors and crew of the film 'Hatari', currently being shot locally starring John Wayne, Elsa Martinelli and Hardy Kruger. Clad in filthy clothes (no change of clothing), decorated with garlands of everlasting flowers in honour of our conquest of the mountain, doubtless far from pleasing on the nose (no showers or baths for five days), and barefoot (we had removed our shoes and socks on arrival at the van, and our feet were much too blistered and swollen for them to be put back on again), we wandered in, a noisome rabble, to the august lobby of the Safari Hotel where we plumped ourselves down in the armchairs and ordered Cokes all round. When the waiter brought them, we asked if it was possible to speak to Mr John Wayne. We were friends of his, we explained, here from America. The waiter, ever courteous, went away and came back a short time later to report that unfortunately this would be impossible since Mr Wayne was out shooting on location and would not be back until later. Did we wish to leave a message? Certainly, we said. Tell him that Mr Eisenhower called. However, this was a well-read waiter, and his face splitting into a grin he wagged his finger roguishly at us and said "Oh no! That is your President!" So off we had to go without ever having met The Duke.

On top of Africa! I felt as sick as I look!

The tone and character of a school is very often set by its Principal, and this was certainly true of the Duke of York when I first went there. The Headmaster was George "Pansy" James, whose nickname was derived from his cherubic physiognomy, chubby pink cheeks beneath grand-fatherly white hair. His appearance could not have been more misleading: Pansy was a man of iron; feared and respected by staff and students alike. He did a tremendous job in forging a completely new school, creating not only the physical fabric of the organisation, but that indefinable spirit and identity that, by the time I joined it less than ten years into its existence, had given the school its unique and special ethos. Pansy retired at the end of 1959, to be succeeded by Victor Laing, who came to us from Falcon College in Southern Rhodesia (as it then was), a decent and likeable man who never really succeeded in filling his predecessor's giant shoes.

Schoolwork naturally dominated our lives at school, but there were plenty of distractions, apart from those already mentioned.

Many people learned musical instruments (not me, alas) and there was an excellent choir under the baton of the choirmaster and music teacher, Jimmy Gordon. Jimmy was a lean and energetic young man who had come to us after 6 years teaching at Eton. He set high standards and, under his direction, the choir earned an enviable reputation. Apart from the usual hymns, we sang choral works such as Handel's 'Messiah' and many other less well-known pieces. I joined the choir as a treble and spent a brief period as an alto before finding my final resting place as a bass. As well as running the choir, Jimmy was responsible for producing the musicals that the school frequently staged, beginning with 'HMS Pinafore' in 1959. The principal female roles (Buttercup the Bumboat Woman, and the Captain's daughter) were filled by outside women, but all the rest of the cast were boys, including the host of Sir Joseph Porter's sisters, cousins, and aunts. I played the Chief S, C & A, Cousin Hebe, whose only solo singing line was in Sir Joseph's first song when I had to echo after each verse "And so do his sisters and his cousins and his aunts!" My role as a female, with a handsome candy-striped gown, drew a good deal of ragging from the other boys, who called me Cousin Bibi ('*bibi*' being Kiswahili for 'woman') but it was mostly fairly good-natured. Of much greater concern was the fact that, by the time production week arrived, my voice had begun to break, and my solo line, which was pitched at a fairly high level, was stretching my vocal capacity to its limit. I tried to solve the problem by lubricating my vocal chords with cold tea behind the scenes, and in the end managed to get through without cracking, but it was a worrying time.

HMS Pinafore 1959 CD in centre with Admiral Sir Joseph Porter

Jimmy Gordon was a G & S fan, and my final appearance on the stage at the Duko was as the Pirate King in 'The Pirates of Penzance'. This is a marvellous, swash-buckling, role and, unfettered by peer-group ridicule or hormonal changes, I could give it my all. If my performance was less memorable than Jon English's classic rendering of recent years, I can offer in part mitigation the fact that in 1962 the copyright to all the Savoy Operas was still held by the D'Oyly Carte Opera Company, who insisted that no changes or modifications to the plays be made; you produced it the way Gilbert and Sullivan had written it, or you did not produce it at all!

My other significant stage performance at the school was in 'Macbeth', where I played Malcolm, the elder of the murdered King Duncan's sons, who returned at last to defeat Macbeth. In between that and the Pirates was a significant stage event, although in the end I did not take part in the staging of it. One of my friends and classmates, also in Delamere House, was a boy called Martin Attwood. He was an extraordinarily talented person, a good runner, a fine soccer and hockey goalkeeper, and academically well above average. His dominant characteristic was an amazing determination; when he set his mind to do something, it usually got done. His greatest talents were creative. He was an excellent trumpeter and succeeded the afore-mentioned 'Minnie' Amos as the leader of the school dance band. He had a fine tenor voice and had immersed himself in the music of the leading tenors of the day, and it was through him that I came to know and appreciate the work of such as Richard Tauber, Beniamino Gigli, and Jussi Bjorling. He was also a first-rate artist, who contributed many drawings and cartoons to the School Annual, "The Yorkist" and the occasionally-produced school newspaper, "The Brooklands Baraza". I still have, framed above my desk, a wonderful little drawing he did of a Hun, fresh from Attila's Tour of Europe. Marty and I were both G & S fans (he played the Major-General in the Pirates) and between us we wrote a comic opera, Marty doing the music and I the book and lyrics. This musical, entitled "Infernal Combustion", had a plot of suitably Gilbertian absurdity centred around the love between the handsome son of the blacksmith and the lovely daughter of the villainous motor-car trader, Sli-mio Polio, whose smelly and noisy product was seeking to usurp the noble horse from English village life. It was produced by the School in the first term of 1961 to rave reviews. I should have had a leading role but, for some reason I can no longer remember, had a falling out with Jimmy Gordon, the producer, threw a wobbly, and walked off the set. They evidently got on very well without me! Marty and I wrote another comic opera next year, but it was never produced, ostensibly because we ran out of time for a full production, though I suspect it may just not have been as good as our first attempt. Excerpts from this musical, whose name I can no longer recall, were sung before the school, so our efforts were not entirely wasted.

The Pirates of Penzance 1962 Marty Attwood is the General in the middle

My reputation as a writer of musicals led to an invitation from a local theatrical identity to write a revue for young people, which I did together with a girl called Norah Hutchison. "The Coffee Bar Revue" played several nights to appreciative audiences at the little puppet theatre near the Nairobi Arboretum where I had gone so often with Ma during her days as Girl Guide Commissioner. Norah and I wrote and performed in a second revue, based on the Wild West theme, called the "Saloon Bar Revue", which also did well. Revue was a very prevalent form of theatre at that time, ranging from Flanders and Swann's delightfully witty "At the drop of a hat" through the mad-cap satire of "Beyond the Fringe" to the amazing South African revue "Wait a Minim" which, after transferring from Johannesburg, played at the Fortune Theatre in London's West End for several years from 1961. One of the stars of 'Wait a Minim' was a young Englishman called Jeremy Taylor, and one of his numbers from the show, "Agh pleez deddy!" (The ballad of the southern suburbs) was top of the Kenya hit parade for months and received so much air time that some disc jockeys refused to play it because they were so fed up with hearing it.

As at Pembroke House, our exeats from the Duko were normally limited to three per term, only one of which was over night. However, there were many other opportunities for escape if you wished to take them. Twice a week, on Wednesday and Thursday afternoons, the school truck would drive into Nairobi. You could obtain permission to go in and, dressed in your best (white shirt, tie, blazer, and trilby hat) could spend a couple of hours wandering around town, perhaps meeting girls at the Thorn Tree Café, or the Rendezvous, before boarding the truck for the journey home. Prefects would often ride into town on their bikes and catch the truck home – riding back to school was mostly up hill: much harder work! I took advantage of the weekly city runs to start my first business. I would go into town and make my way to a little Indian food store in Bazaar Street where I had an arrangement with the owner. I would purchase from him an insulated box containing 100 samozas, crisp, spicy and delicious, at a price of 25 cents each and take them back to school where I sold them for 50 cents. This theoretically gave me a profit of 25 shillings a week, big money in 1960. Unfortunately, I ate or gave away so much of the product that I very seldom netted anything like that!

One matter which occupied our minds a great deal of the time was – girls: how to meet them and how to 'get off' with them ('getting off', I might add, usually meaning nothing more than some breathless snogging in the dark at a dance). As boarders at an all-boys school, of course, we had more problems with this than the average boy, but in fact there were plenty of ways of solving these. One was to get involved in activities which, by their nature, entailed contact with the girls' schools. These included Scottish Country Dancing and Square Dancing, which had dances with one or other of the main girl's schools several times a year. Even better was the Young Farmers Association which would not only get together with their female counterparts for workshops and discussions on such gripping topics as wool classing, butterfat measurement, and crop rotation, but could also expect to spend several mornings working at the Royal Show.

The Royal Show was one of the great annual events of colonial Kenya. Held at Mitchell (later Jamhuri) Park, a wooded showground off the Ngong Road not far from the school, in October every year, it was a time when all the people from 'up-country' and their animals would descend upon Nairobi for a week of catching up with old friends, drinking, whinging about the Government, circulating the latest scandals, and generally having a good time. The Young Farmers were employed to help look after the prize livestock down for the Show and lead them around the Show ring and in the subsequent Grand Parade. There was plenty of time for fraternising with the Young Farmers from the girls' schools away from the cattle pens, and always lots of interesting stalls to visit, free samples to be sought, and food to be eaten. Although I was never a Young Farmer, I usually managed to spend longer at the Show than the single day that was the allowance for other non-Farmer students. This was because Pa was, for many years, the Chief Steward of the Show, and Tony and I often used to go along with him and help by running errands, taking messages, and similar menial tasks. Apart from the commercial stalls, side-shows, and the livestock, there was a full programme of events in the main arena, including sheep dog trials, police dog demonstrations, tent-pegging, stunt driving and other exciting and exotic happenings. One of my favourite events was the show jumping, of which there was plenty in the arena every day. I loved the horses with their glowing coats and thundering hooves, snorting through wide nostrils as they strained to lift themselves and their riders over extremely solid fences that seemed as tall as I was. I can still remember one of the champion jumpers, a lion-hearted little grey mare called Djinnesta, who flew over the fences with deceptive ease, her long white tail flowing free behind her.

The highlight in the arena, however, was the final event on the programme on the last evening, the Beating of the Retreat by the Massed Bands. The bands included those of the Kenya Police and the King's African Rifles (KAR) plus those from whatever British Regiments happened to be in Kenya at the time. When the moment came, the arena had been completely cleared and the fence at one end dismantled to provide wide access. The lights in the stadium would suddenly shut off, leaving us all in total darkness and silence, broken only by the muffled shuffling of feet as the bandsmen manoeuvred into place. Then through the gloom the disembodied voice of the Band Major would be heard. "Massed bands! By the centaaah – quick maaarch!!" and on the first roll of drums the lights would snap on to reveal the serried ranks of bandsmen marching into the arena to a rousing Souza tune, the light sparkling on the silver and gold of their trumpets, trombones and tubas, the red tunics and bearskins of the Guards contrasting with the Colobus-skin shakoes and green tunics of the KAR. It was a spine-tingling sight and a fitting end to what was always a magical week.

In addition to opportunities for inter-gender contact afforded by Scottish Dancing and the like, there were occasional school dances or 'hops' to which you could invite a girl if you had progressed that far along the thorny road. The girls' schools too had such hops, and there was always hope that you might score an invitation to one. There were several European girls' high schools in Kenya at that time, but the two most significant were the Kenya Girls' High School in Nairobi and the Limuru Girls School at (surprise) Limuru. The Kenya Girls' High School was otherwise known as the Heifer Boma, or the Boma for short (a *boma* is a thorny enclosure used for the protection of cattle and other livestock). Situated, as the vulture flies, not many miles from us, it was a large mainly boarding school which tried to protect its students' virtue by requiring them to wear an extraordinarily unbecoming uniform of a shapeless grey skirt, white blouse, and flat shoes. It was a tribute to their femininity (and our lust) that so many of them were able to rise above this handicap and form mutually satisfactory relationships with students from the neighbouring boys' schools (The Boma was conveniently sited within easy reach of all of the main boys' boarding schools, the Duke of York, Prince of Wales, and St. Mary's, the Catholic boys school). The Limuru Girls School was much smaller and more remote, located in lush green woodland a few miles short of Limuru in the highlands north of Nairobi. Perhaps because they were much less accessible, Limuru Girls had a bit more of a cachet than Boma women (your regular girlfriend, to whom you would be said to be 'hitched' was described as your 'woman', even if she was only 14!). There were, of course, other schools, a Loreto Convent at Msongari near Nairobi and the Delamere High School, a coeducational day high school founded quite soon after I went to the Duko, and we would occasionally fraternise with their denizens, but there weren't quite the same ties.

The Kenya High School was a remarkable institution ruled with a rod of iron by the Headmistress of many years Miss "Jamy" Stott (no, I don't know, but I doubt if it is edifying). Its academic standards were extraordinarily high and a source of frequent invidious comparison by our teachers when commenting on our efforts, and Jamy would go to great lengths to protect this reputation. It was said that when the School Certificate results were received, early in the January term each year, on the rare occasions when girls had failed the exam (and been unwise enough to return to the school for the following year), these unhappy creatures would be taken aside beforehand and sent off to the sanatorium to recover so that Jamy could get up at assembly and announce "Girls! The School Certificate results have been received and I am delighted to be able to say that no-one in this room has failed!" In the sixties, Ma worked at the Boma for several years as the Careers Secretary and in that capacity met my future wife, Shirley, several years before I did. She was also therefore able, when Shirley and I started going out seriously, to go back and check my beloved's file to make sure she was a suitable companion for her eldest son (verdict, apparently, 'yes'). The whole atmosphere at Limuru, despite having at that time the daughter of the Archbishop of Canterbury as Headmistress, was a good deal less daunting and serious.

The year after I had successfully completed my School Certificate, the time came around again for the family to enjoy a spot of 'home leave'. As in 1954, my father was given nearly six months off with pay and we made ready to fly north again. Once more, Tony and I missed a whole term of school, but my parents doubtless argued that we would learn just as much on our European holiday, albeit of slightly different things, and that, being quite bright, we could soon catch up. At all events, no objection was raised, and I do not even remember being required to do any study while we were away. So it was that for the second time in our lives, our house and pets were handed over to strangers, warm clothes were dug out of storage, and we exchanged Nairobi's reliable sunshine for the uncertainties of an English spring.

Tony and I off to school 1960

Chapter 6

Last years at school

The England we found in 1961 was certainly different from the one we had visited in 1954. The era of post-war austerity had been replaced by increasing national prosperity. The Prime Minister of the day, Harold Macmillan (alias 'Supermac'), had told Britons that they had never had it so good. (Contemporary joke: A woman rushes into a police station to report that she has just been raped. "Any clues as to the identity of your assailant?" asks the Duty Sergeant. "I'm not sure," replies the woman "but I think it might have been Harold Macmillan." "Really, Madam? What makes you think that?" "Well, I've never had it so good!" Ho ho). Swinging London, Mary Quant, David Hockney, the mini-skirt, and the Beatles were just around the corner. Alec Issigonis had revolutionised the small car market by inventing the Mini.

Six amazing months flew by – test cricket at Lord's and the Oval, a grand European tour, more getting to know the relatives. Then, as the English summer reached its end, we too came to the conclusion of our long holiday and flew south, via Rome, to take up once more the threads of normal life in a Kenya now destined, by decree of British Colonial Secretary Ian Macleod, to be self-governing within a year and independent before the end of 1963.

I suppose that for most people the last couple of years at school tend to be the most rewarding and enjoyable. You are at or near the top of the tree, you can bask in the privileges of seniority, such as they may be, and it will be the time of your greatest achievement in whatever fields of endeavour you compete in. On the other hand, of course, it is also the time when the pressure of the final examinations is upon you. I don't remember this being the all-consuming obsession which so many of our final year schoolboys and girls are encouraged to develop these days, although there is no doubt that we took our studies seriously. The School Chaplain, a little dark-faced Welshman called Rev. Bennett-Rees known to all as "Charlie" ('Charlie Chaplain' – get it? Very droll) told us that we would have to do a minimum of 5 hours study a day if we wanted to have any hope at all of getting into a decent university. This sowed a seed of doubt in my mind, because I was certainly not doing anything like that amount of work, but I didn't regard the Chaplain as a very trustworthy person so did not allow this seed to grow into anything likely to spoil the even tenor of my existence.

The 5th and 6th forms were the stages of progress through the school at which you might expect to start to assume leadership roles, and at the beginning of 1961 I was appointed one of several House Prefects in Delamere. This gave me an extra bar on the cuffs of my blazer, the right to have and ride a bike (a 'grid') at school, and the appointment of a couple of 'rabble' as my personal batmen. My chief rabble was a little boy called Alexander Temple, a dark-haired lad with the peachy complexion and demure manner of a choirboy (which he was). When reproved for some misdemeanour, he would lower his incredibly long lashes onto his cheeks with such an air of injured innocence that it was impossible to remain angry with him for long. Behind this angelic exterior, however, lurked a very tough kid who had no problems lording it over his peers. The previous year had seen the opening of the two new boarding houses, Grogan and James, and volunteers had been called for to transfer to those houses. For us fourth formers there was, at least in our minds, the possibility that we might thereby get early promotion to the school aristocracy, and no doubt that influenced some decisions. Although tempted, I decided to stay where I was. Our Head of House in 1961 was Jay Daubeney, a popular boy with spectacles and rather bad acne. He was an excellent sportsman and, despite his volcanic face, a considerable ladies man. His predecessor in Delamere House was Michael "Monkey" Johnson, a stalwart of the 1st XV and another very popular and respected leader. Monkey's reign came to a sudden end just two days before speech day in his last term. The Head, Mr Laing, received a phone call late at night from the Headmistress of Limuru Girls School. Limuru had broken up a day or two before us but some of their girls were still in residence waiting for trains to go up-country. They had gone AWOL and the word was that they had been seen in one of Nairobi's night spots with boys rumoured to be from the Duke of York. Mr Laing immediately went to find the Head of School, Colin Brooks, who was in Thomson House, part of Block I with Delamere, to see if he could shed any light on the matter. Lo and behold - no Colin! The Head went to the next door House to see Monkey Johnson. Another empty bed! Colin, Monkey and two other senior boys were expelled, and a genial soul called Charlie Kean became Head Boy for the last two days of school.

A leadership role I had never expected was thrust upon me when I returned to school after missing that term we had spent on leave in Europe. Cricket was definitely my strongest game. I had been captain of the junior colts in my second year at the school, in which we had been very successful, mainly as a result of the bowling of a lanky Irish boy called Tony Maguire. Maguire was a natural athlete, big for his age, and frighteningly quick. I used to field at very short square leg to his bowling, and between us we claimed many a scalp as terrified batsmen desperately fended off short deliveries aimed at the body. The only downside to this partnership as far as I was concerned was that Maguire had what he fondly imagined was a very effective slower ball which he would occasionally bowl without forewarning me. The only thing one could say about this ball was that it was, indeed, very slow! Batsmen who had been cowering under a lethal barrage would seize upon this gentle dolly-drop with relieved glee, sending the close-in fieldsman (me) diving for cover.

The next year Maguire went straight into the 1st XI and I captained the Senior Colts (under 16 years and 2 months). Although I had a couple of games for the 1st XI towards the end of the season – the school would often 'blood' up-and-coming players in some of the matches against clubs – and was reasonably hopeful of making the top team in 1961, I was as amazed as anyone to be called in by the Master in Charge of Cricket, Mr Harry Hesketh, and be told that he had a job for me – Captain of Cricket! It was certainly a bold step and one which, in the short term at least, did not really pay off. I think my appointment was resented by some of the older boys, and I did not have the maturity to deal with this as well as the pressures of Captaincy. We did not have a specially good season and lost most of the important games.

Our main rivals, at cricket as in other sports, were The Prince of Wales and the Catholic boys' school, St Mary's. St Mary's was somewhat smaller than us, but they had an awesome sporting reputation. The Brothers liked to win – I think they saw it as vindication of their religious dogma, proof that God was definitely on their side – and not only did they instill the fiercest competitive spirit in their students but they were apt, where necessary, to act as the arm of the Lord when His servants needed a little help. In matches against St Mary's your chance of being given 'not out' in response to appeals for LBW or caught behind was slim indeed if one of the Brothers was standing umpire.

That first year of my Captaincy St Mary's had a trump card in the form of a fearsome quick bowler called Chris Gazzard. Not only was he quick but he could swing the ball several feet both ways, and our first game against them was a disaster when we were bowled out for about 40; the only person to reach double figures being me for a doggedly defensive dozen or so runs. The outstanding player in the Prince of Wales side was a lad called Keith McAdam, the son of an academic at Makerere University in Uganda. Keith was an accomplished left-hand batsman whose career paralleled mine to an extraordinary degree. He went to Kenton College, Pembroke House's deadly rival, and after the Prince of Wales, where we were again opposing Captains, he went to Cambridge while I went to Oxford. Keith was a far better cricketer than I was, however, and got his Blue for the sport at Cambridge, captaining the University in his last year there.

Although that first year of senior cricket was a disappointment in many ways, there were compensations. The school games were always keenly fought (as well as the Prince of Wales and St Mary's, we also played the Duke of Gloucester School, one of the chief Asian secondary schools) but the most enjoyable matches were the ones we played against a number of the clubs, some of them outside Nairobi, such as Limuru, Machakos, or Thika. These were played on a Sunday, and we would be transported out there by the school truck. The school did not have a bus as such, just a truck like an army lorry with benches round the sides, a solid roof, and canvas screens at the side which could be rolled up out of the way if desired. The roof had a 10-inch lip around it, presumably to facilitate the carriage of baggage on top, and when coming back at night from such excursions as a dance up at Limuru, we would often climb up there and lie on our backs smoking or just looking at the stars.

The Club games were fun for a number of reasons. It was always good to get away from school for a day, and there was generally an excellent lunch and afternoon tea to break the day up. Best of all, we were allowed to drink 'shandies' (beer and lemonade) which always put a rosy glow on matters. The journey back to school in the truck through the twilight was always accompanied by raucous singing, while those whose bladders were a little overwhelmed by the volume of shandy consumed could relieve themselves through a hole that had thoughtfully been provided in the floor of the truck. The year ended on a good note for me with my selection (the only one from The Duke of York) in the Combined Schools side for the annual match against the Kenya Kongonis and the winning of my cricket Colours, which gave me the right to have silver piping sewn around the border of my blazer. Neither of these distinctions was universally acclaimed, there being many who thought that I did not deserve them.

The 1962 cricket season was a much happier one from every point of view; I was more mature and sensible, those most resentful of my leadership had gone, and we had unprecedented success, beating St Mary's and the Delamere School, and only being foiled from whitewashing the Prince of Wales after thrashing them in the first fixture when their last pair of batsmen hung on for a draw in the return game. I got my bête noire Keith McAdam out cheaply in both games, and was again picked for the Combined Schools, this time as Captain in the absence of Keith who could not play for some reason. My opening knock of 41 helped the Combined Schools to a rare victory over the Kongonis. Our successful season was reflected in the awarding of Colours to the entire team (which included my brother Tony), a most unusual event. As a cautionary aside at this point, I might mention that one of the most embarrassing experiences of my life was associated with cricket. Just after the end of my final term, another young player from the Duke of York, Ian Shields, and I were selected to play in a Kongonis invitation side in a two-day game up at Nyeri. We were put up at the house of the District Commissioner, a Major Gay, whom I knew from Pembroke House days because his son Nigel had been a contemporary there. On the Saturday evening of the match Mrs Gay took Ian and me to a barbecue round at the house of a local dignitary where I proceeded to get totally and shamefully drunk, beginning the evening on brandy-and-ginger, at that time my 'tipple of choice', then progressing to brandy and soda when the ginger ran out and ending with straight brandy. I was apparently found unconscious on the back lawn when it was time to go home and was carried to the DC's Mercedes where I revived sufficiently to be sick all over the back seat. I woke the next day, with a head surprisingly clear as a bell (at least I hadn't mixed my drinks!) but with a very vivid recollection of just what I had done. They had left the car untouched for me to clean up but were otherwise very kind about the affair. I, however, was consumed with shame and guilt, and not just because of what the Gays and their friends might think of me. One of the other guests at the barbecue was a woman called Peggy Towers who was a close Guiding friend of Ma's, and I was certain that the news of my disgrace must find its way through her back to my parents. For weeks the thought of this hung like a cloud over me, but evidently Mrs Towers was kinder than I deserved, for I never heard any more about it. I have never drunk brandy since, and even the smell of it turns my stomach!

Duko Cricket 1ˢᵗ XI 1962
Back row: Tony Durrant, Peter Dunt, Bruce McIver, George Marston, Ian
Shields, Hugh Aldous
Front row: Dave Hutchison, John Dunt, CD, Bryce Cowan, Rusty Ballard
Both Dunts went on to become Admirals in the Royal Navy

Sporting success at school for me was largely confined to the cricket pitch. I was never much good at hockey, the official sport in term one, and I took the view that, if the Lord had wanted me to swim, he would have given me webbed feet. It is ironic, in view of my passionate devotion to the game over the past 50 years or so, that I was not especially successful at, nor particularly keen on, rugby while at school. I had two years in, first, the Junior, then the Senior Colts, but missed the 1961 season because of being in England. Prior to the 1962 season I did some extra pre-season training down at Nondescripts RFC for whom I later played but my hopes that this would give me an inside run into the school 1ˢᵗ

XV were soon dashed. In fact I didn't even initially make it into the 1st XXX squad from whom the two senior teams were chosen, though my performance in a couple of House matches saw me promoted, and I ended up playing the rest of the season in the 2nd XV. I could console myself now (though of course could not do so then) with the thought that World Cup-winning Wallaby Captain, Nick Farr-Jones didn't make the 1st XV at school either, though I suspect that the competition at his school would have been a good deal more intense than it was at mine.

The school had several tennis courts and a squash court, although inter-school competition was not as keen as in the other sports. For a while I had tennis coaching with a man called Stan Tudor, who was also a gun squash player. Stan was a fitness fanatic who always kept his body in peak condition. Years later, when I was working for the CDC in Nairobi and he was courting one of our secretaries, a lass called Christine Batchelor whom he eventually married, Stan, then in his early 40s, would come up to see her on the 5th floor, eschewing the lift and running up the stairs, arriving scarcely out of breath. The school had its own version of Stan on the staff in the person of the PT Master, Dennis Cooper, a bronzed he-man with a magnificent physique, whose handsome, tanned visage was customarily split by a savage, dazzlingly-white, grin. Dennis was also a good squash player, and he and Stan had many battles in the local championships. My own introduction to the game of squash was in the school's single court, beginning an association with the game that happily continues, nearly 60 years later.

As I have previously indicated, sport was by no means the only extra-curricular activity at school, and many of the things people got up to were well outside even the official extra-curriculum. The considerable areas of bush within the school grounds, apart from providing shelter for worshippers of the demon tobacco, constituted a habitat for a wide variety of wildlife, and hence were a fruitful field for naturalists. We had two lads in Delamere, Scarse and Start, inseparable companions who were animal fanatics, and used to capture some of the denizens of the bush (mainly tree hyraxes) in their box traps. One Sunday morning we were all awakened by an awful screaming from outside the dormitory which, on investigation, turned out to be coming from the trap that Scarse and Start had left there after retrieving it from the bush during the night. The occupant of the box, more than a little irritated at his confinement, was a huge white-tailed mongoose, the largest of his kind, about the size of a kelpie but a great deal more savage, with a bushy white tail at one end and razor-sharp teeth at the other. Mr Spencer had been roused as well as we had and had no hesitation in ordering that the white-tail be returned to the bush without delay.

Some students were more technically inclined. In my second year two of the senior boys, Wallington and Cridland, set up the Delamere Broadcasting Service. This transmitted an interesting programme of news, interviews, and music from a locker in the senior dormitory, and could be received all over the school and sometimes even more widely than that given the vagaries of radio waves. It provided great entertainment for several days until the school authorities decided that it needed to be closed down before somebody at the Kenya Broadcasting Service picked up the signal and started an embarrassing investigation.

The other process that was well under way by the time I began my penultimate year at school was puberty. I was not an especially precocious youth in this regard and, being a year younger than most of my classmates, could not be expected to develop an interest in the other sex as quickly as they did, but the environmental factors ensured that I was not far behind. Then as now, popular music played its part, and we listened every Sunday to the 20 best sellers of the Hit Parade broadcast from England via the local station, "based on the sales of sheet music in the previous week" (a criterion that always mystified me – who on earth ever bought sheet music?). Cliff Richard ('Living doll', 'Travelling light') did battle with Elvis Presley ('Heartbreak hotel', 'Blue suede shoes'), Connie Francis, Tab Hunter, Pat Boone, Clarence 'Frogman' Henry, Jerry Lee Lewis and many more. "Love", often unrequited, was the theme of almost all these songs, which gave an edge and a focus to the scarcely-understood hormonal stirrings within us. Naturally somewhat shy around girls, it was a long time before I was able to translate my urges into any sort of action. I suffered a huge amount of ragging following one dance at the Delamere Girls School where, having inveigled a buxom young blonde called Daphne outside the hall, I was unable to pluck up the courage to do more than sit next to her on a bench in the dark and talk about the forthcoming School Certificate exams!

My first real girl-friend was Sue Solly, a tall, no-nonsense girl with a romantic streak and a great sense of humour, from the Boma. She was the youngest of three daughters of a coffee farmer at Kiambu, near Nairobi. Sue was not petite or glamourous, but she was great fun and I was besotted with her. In her company I attended the round of teenage parties in the Nairobi area over the 1960/61 Christmas season, including celebrating

New Year's Eve at the Ruiru Club, where I recall an embittered old coffee farmer, the recent perfidy of the British Government fresh in his mind, responding to the royal toast by standing up and pledging: "The Queen! God bless her! And damnation to her ministers!" The average teenage party in those days followed a fairly predictable formula, with dancing to the latest tunes in the early part of the evening and then a buffet dinner with fruit punch and other soft drinks. Alcohol was never provided by the hosts and very seldom, in my experience, brought along by the guests. I remember one party when a boy, rather older, but well known to most of us, did arrive very drunk, what a thrill of excitement and horror it sent through the assembly. Later in the evening, the lights would be dimmed or even (depending how vigilant the host parents were), turned off, Ray Conniff would be placed on the turntable, and we would cling to each other on the dance floor as we swayed to his gentle melodies, or sneaked out into the garden for some more serious snogging. It was all pretty innocent stuff. If you had been able to "get off" with a girl at one of these parties, she might become your official girlfriend and you were said to be 'hitched' a fact that might be attested by the exchange of a ring or, more usually, elephant-hair bracelets which were very commonly worn. Back at school, you would write to each other at least once a week (this was before email, Best Beloved!) and the mail delivery would be eagerly awaited so that you could claim the scented blue envelope, shrug off the good-natured jeers of your mates, and take it away somewhere private to read and re-read every precious word.

Now that social life had taken on a new dimension, mobility in the holidays became more of a problem. Both my parents still worked, Pa now the Kenya Prisons Welfare Officer (concerned with the welfare of the warders, not the prisoners: no-one worried too much about them) and Ma as previously mentioned as the Careers Secretary at the Kenya High School. I had always wanted to get a motor-bike – my dream was a BSA Bantam, but it was the era of the motor scooter and, having reached my 16th birthday I was bought a second-hand 125 cc Vespa. Passing the test to get the licence for this caused me some anxiety because of my short sightedness, at that time a secret guarded by me from everyone. I had heard that the test for your eyes consisted of being asked to read a number-plate about 25 yards away, and I spent several minutes before the test outside the licensing centre trying to memorise the number plates of all the cars parked around. In the end I had no reason to worry: I don't think I was actually asked to read anything at all, and a brief ride up and down the car-park under the bored eyes of the examiner saw me ticked off as competent and licensed to kill. The scooter opened a whole new world to me and although not suitable for travelling outside the Nairobi area (with its small wheels and high centre of gravity it was absolutely lethal on slippery surfaces) it enabled me to visit town, friends' houses, the swimming pool and many other places without any problem. During term-time, Ma used the Vespa to go to and from her work at the Kenya High, a somewhat unusual means of transport that I suspect did a good deal for what one would now call her 'street cred'.

Much of our holidays were spent socialising or just 'mucking around' at home. However, from time to time there would be a family excursion, usually to the game parks or the coast. East Africa then, as now, was home to many of the world's most exciting wild animals, and its game parks were justly famous. The Nairobi National Park was right on our doorstep with its main gate at Langata not far, as the crow flies, from the Duke of York school. One of my earliest memories is of staying with my Uncle Peter, then still with the KAR, at his house in the army camp at Langata and seeing lions from the park wandering through the camp. Lions were the only one of the 'Big Five' commonly found in the park in those days, although rhino were occasionally seen and leopard were no doubt there, but the place teemed with plains game – wildebeeste, hartebeeste, Thomson's and Grant's gazelle, impala, giraffe, zebra, warthog and many more. Lion was what most people came to see and you would drive slowly around the open plains until a distant collection of vehicles would tell you that a pride had been located and you would hasten there to join the crowd of onlookers. We also visited Amboseli, in the shadow of Mount Kilimanjaro, Tsavo and the famous Treetops Hotel, across the clearing from the original tree dwelling in which Princess Elizabeth had received the news of the death of her father King George and her consequent accession to the throne. This original hotel had been burned down by the Mau Mau soon after the Princess' stay. Actually getting to the hotel was one of the most exciting parts of the visit. Having been transported by bus from the Outspan Hotel in Nyeri to a drop-off point in the forest about ½ mile from Treetops, we were escorted by a white hunter, correctly attired in faded khaki safari jacket and shorts and stained veldt hat with leopard-skin hatband, cautiously through the forest. From time to time our escort would pause and stand silently listening, rifle at the ready, while we stood, hearts hammering in our ears, eyeing the closest of the ladders that were nailed to trees at regular intervals for us to rush up if anything dangerous happened on the scene. Satisfied, apparently, that it was safe to continue, he waved us on and we proceeded once more, eyes darting left and right for any sign of life, ears straining for the crash in the undergrowth or the angry snort that might herald the arrival of a buffalo, rhino or elephant. At last we reached the hotel, built into the top of a massive tree with additional supporting wooden pillars, and climbed the steps up into its welcoming bosom, these steps being winched up after us to discourage unwanted visitors. I have no doubt that this whole procedure was a charade: wild animals were unlikely to be moving around in the middle of the afternoon, and the Treetops staff evidently took good care to check out the area before each new batch of visitors arrived. However, it was exciting and set the scene for what was usually a wonderful night's entertainment.

Treetops was situated in the forest of the Aberdare mountain range next to a large water hole and a natural saltlick, which was artificially augmented from time to time to ensure that it continued to be attractive to the local animals. The show would usually begin as dusk fell and, if you had the staying power, could continue all night, under the artificial moon of the hotel's floodlights. For those with less stamina, there were beds, and we were served a magnificent dinner in a dining room opening out onto one of the viewing balconies, so that diners could move over to viewing mode if anything unusual turned up during the meal. Buffalo, elephant, waterbuck and bushbuck were common visitors to the waterhole, and you might be lucky enough to see a rhino or a leopard or, if really fortunate, one of those rare and shy inhabitants of the jungle such as the bongo, okapi, or giant forest hog. Rather less welcome visitors were the baboons to whom, of course, a retractable staircase posed no barrier at all, and who would hang around the viewing platform on the lookout for opportunities. The tourists were, naturally, enjoined not to feed them, but this did not mean the baboons went hungry. They were skilled 'bag-snatchers' and you could not leave any possessions, edible or not, unattended if you wished to keep them. I had a large slab of Old English toffee that I was eating and put down for a moment on the railing of the observation platform while I studied something on the far edge of the waterhole through my binoculars and a hairy hand swooped in with lightning speed and bore it away. I don't know how a baboon would have coped with a slab of toffee - their teeth are not really designed for that sort of food – but I dare say he would have found a way!

Trying to not feed the baboons at Treetops

Fishing was another pastime we occasionally indulged in. Pa had always been a keen fly fisherman, and many of the streams and rivers in the Kenya highlands were stocked with rainbow trout. The end of the Emergency meant that it was again safe to fish these rivers, and we made several expeditions to fish the Theba and Sagana Rivers on Mount Kenya and up on the Kinangop west of the Aberdares. We also spent a week once fishing the Suam River in north-western Kenya beyond Eldoret towards the Uganda border. The trouble with these expeditions was that, except in the areas very remote from human settlement which were difficult to get to (that's why they were 'remote'!), these rivers were severely poached, so that the few fish remaining in them were wild and wily. In terms of results, therefore, fishing in these rivers was not rewarding, especially for tyro anglers such as we were. However, it was beautiful country, the gentle gurgle of the streams as they wended their way through the cool forest was soothing, and we caught a fish often enough to maintain our interest (Usually: I do recall, however, the three of us, with Ma as non-playing captain, fishing the Suam River for 5 days and catching only one trout, and that one illegally on a spinner!). We also on two occasions tried our hand at deep-sea fishing off Malindi when we were staying there. The first time it was rather rough, I was wretchedly sea-sick, and the catch for the whole boat was one smallish barracuda. The second time we went out, a year or two later, we had the good fortune to strike a 'run' of sailfish. They were taking everything we threw in the water. At one time we had a fish on every one of the boat's three rods at the same time. We ended up with 5 sailfish, of which my tally was 2, none of them huge (I think my biggest weighed about 70 lbs.), but definitely worth the trouble and cost.

My first trout c.1959

The coast remained a favourite holiday destination, though we usually went south of Mombasa to Diani rather than north to Malindi. One school holidays my Housemaster, Mr Spencer, invited me and one of my classmates, Rob Bradshaw, to accompany his family for a week to Diani where they had rented a house. This placed Rob and me in a very awkward situation: on the one hand it seemed churlish to turn down the offer of a free holiday while on the other, if we accepted we would have to face endless ragging from our fellows at school ("Hey! Durrant! Your father-in-law wants to see you" etc). In the end and doubtless with a bit of parental pressure, I suppose we could not think of any good reason why we shouldn't go and so we did. The party consisted of the Spencers, parents and three daughters, a middle-aged family friend called Patrick Moore who insisted on being called by his nickname Orless (Moore or less – get it?) and a very attractive French lass from Madagascar called Marie-France Bec. Rob and I immediately fell in lust with Marie-France and did our best to win her favours. We were, however, wasting our time. At 19 years of age, M-F was not in the least turned on by the sexual charms of callow teenagers such as we, and in any case she was saving herself for Prince Baudouin of Belgium whom she had made up her mind to marry. History tells us, alas, that she missed out there. Despite the disappointment of not making it with M-F, it was a thoroughly enjoyable holiday, as a holiday at the Kenya coast was almost bound to be, and was probably worth the hard time that our kind and sensitive fellow students gave us on our return to school.

1962, my final year at school, was a significant one in many ways. Kenya was moving inexorably through self-government towards full independence. The first cracks in the surface of racial segregation in education had appeared at the Duke of York. Our first Asian students, the Mamujee twins, entered the school in 1961, and the following year saw our first black African, a lad in my House called John Okwirry. Jomo Kenyatta, described by the British Governor at the time of his imprisonment as a "leader into darkness and death" was to be released, a fact that accelerated the emigration plans of many European settlers who envisaged a vengeful bloodbath once Jomo and his henchmen were in control. It is interesting reading the 'Valete' section of the School magazine, 'The Yorkist', for 1962 to see the large number of junior boys who left that year "to school in UK or South Africa". Only the previous year, the first European in Kenya history to be executed for the murder of an African had mounted the scaffold in Kamiti Prison. Peter Poole, a young married man living in a Nairobi suburb, had been so enraged by an African passer-by throwing stones at his barking dog that he had rushed inside, grabbed his gun, and shot the man dead. Fifty years before he might have escaped with his life, but times had changed, fatally for Peter Poole. As you might expect, opinion among the expatriate community was polarised, some wishing to excuse a 'crime of passion' and moved by sympathy for Poole's young wife and family, others saying that he was a fool who only got what he deserved.

On the international scene, nothing impressed me more than the Cuban Missile Crisis, which had us tuning in to the BBC World Service and hanging on every word. For 2 or 3 days I was quite convinced that we were on the brink of World War III and, having just read Neville Shute's "On the beach", Kenya did not seem too remote to be consumed in such a nuclear confrontation.

At school, I had started the year a little disappointed at being overlooked as Head of Delamere and School Prefect – the job went to my good friend Rusty Ballard. However, I don't think my disappointment ran too deep as I am sure that I realised in my heart of hearts that he was a much more suitable person for the job than I was. In the classroom the focus was obviously on preparing for the Higher School Certificate examinations to be sat at the end of the year and, in my case and many others, securing entry to university. Options for tertiary study in Kenya were limited. There was a fairly-recently established University College in Nairobi, affiliated to London University, but it lacked prestige and I suspect the range of courses offered was not wide. Makerere University in Uganda was a well-established school with a good reputation, though mainly in Science rather than the Arts. A few sent their children to complete their studies in South Africa, but the vast majority turned their eyes north to the traditional universities of Britain. One of my class-mates, John "Jog" O'Grady had obtained admission to Magdalen College, Oxford, even without his Higher School Certificate, and he left school at the end of the second term to commence at university in the English autumn. It had been decided that I too should go to Oxford (I am not sure why – perhaps because my cousins Will and Simon were up at Christchurch). I applied to Worcester College, alma mater of my girl-friend Sue's father, (the uninspiring architecture of whose main buildings gave rise to the saying "C'est magnifique, mais ce n'est pas la gare!") and also to Brasenose College (BNC) in both cases to read Modern Languages. I only had one modern language (French) but there was apparently provision for Latin also to be counted as a modern language in certain circumstances. In addition to sitting my Higher School Certificate, I also sat some extremely difficult scholarship papers in French. Then, with the sense of relief, release, and resignation that always comes at the end of a hard bout of concentrated effort, I joined my fellow students on holiday, leaving my fate in the lap of the gods or, to be more accurate, their local agents, the examiners.

1962 was to mark a significant turning point for my family, quite apart from my finishing school and, all being well, going on to university in England. My parents had decided that, after 15 years, the time had come to leave Kenya. No doubt the uncertainties that existed about the Colony's future under an independent black government influenced them, as well as the fact that I would be in England for at least the next three years. Rosemary's husband Jacob, too, had decided to return to Europe, in his case to his native Norway, taking his family with him. So it had been resolved that Tony should do his last two years of schooling in England, and some of our time during home leave in 1961 was spent reviewing possible schools for him. In the end, he was enrolled in Brighton College, to begin in the Lent term of 1963. Assuming I gained admission to Oxford, or some other English university, I was also to leave Kenya early in the new year to go to Paris, where I was to enrol in a 6 month Cours de Civilisation Française at the Sorbonne, before returning to England for a summer holiday preparatory to commencing my university career proper.

Before all of this, though, we were to have a family Christmas, possibly the last one we would enjoy all together for many years. Christmas chez Durrant followed a traditional routine that varied little from year to year. On Christmas Eve we would go to the carol service at our local parish church, St Mark's, initially in the little stone building in Parklands where Rosemary was married, and then in the larger and more functional, though less attractive, church building in Westlands, not far from the primary school. Then it was home to open the presents under the tree. Decorating the tree was, of course, a large part of the build-up to the season, and, in the early years, incredible as it may seem, it was adorned with real candles, set in holders clipped onto the branches, which were lit when we were all around it on Christmas Eve. One year the inevitable eventually happened, and the candles set fire to the tree which, like all good conifers, soon ignited in a merry blaze. Pa had to grab it at the base and rush it out through the front door, hurling it down the steps onto the drive where it burned harmlessly before our shocked eyes. After that we graduated to electric lights! The rest of the house was also decked with tinsel and baubles and one year when Tony and I were still quite small, we had the brilliant idea of specially decorating our room. Countless little Christmas scenes, fir trees, Father Christmases and the like were drawn and coloured in, and then pasted up on the wall. It took us the whole morning, but at the end of it there was hardly a square inch uncovered. When our parents came home for lunch we proudly ushered them into the room and stood back to receive their delighted accolades. As you may imagine, the reaction, especially from Pa, was bewilderingly different from our expectation! The entire room had to have the walls scraped and repainted. Our days of do-it-yourself Christmas decorations were definitely over.

Following the excitement of the presents on Christmas Eve, and the giving of their Christmas hamper to the servants, the adults would settle down for a night-cap while we children scampered off to bed to try and get some sleep before Father Christmas called. Like children everywhere, we doubted we would ever be able to close our eyes but, like children everywhere, we always fell fast asleep, and I cannot remember ever waking to catch Santa at his task. Christmas morning was opening the stockings (usually old stockings of Ma's, invariably with the traditional apple and orange in the toe) and then on with the Sunday best to go off to church for matins. Back home again, and it was a traditional Christmas lunch with ham, turkey, Christmas pudding and brandy butter, and crackers, with champagne for the older members of the party which, by 1962, included Tony and me. The pudding had the traditional symbols – the horn of plenty, the bachelor's button etc. – concealed within it. After lunch, which we sometimes held outside under the jacaranda trees on the front lawn, we would listen to the Queen's speech on the radio and then would often try and ring the family in England, usually at Granny's; a far more laborious and expensive process than it is today. For the rest of the afternoon we would nurse our dyspepsia until tea-time when, for those with some room left in their stomachs (i.e. the younger members of the congregation) the Christmas cake would be cut. Rosemary and Jacob and the two little girls would often join us on Christmas Day, and it was invariably a happy, family occasion. Christmas 1962, though, was perhaps going to be the last of these occasions, and Tony and I made the most of it.

Boxing Day as usual saw us up at the Limuru races, and that year we then had a few days in a camp in the Tsavo National Park, except for Pa who had to work. Calling in at a friend's home on the way back we had an urgent message to ring Pa. A letter had arrived from Oxford. BNC, presumably after carefully studying my scholarship exam, had decided to offer me a place for 1963 to read, not Languages, but Modern History. I didn't care. A surge of elation raced through me. I was in! My course for the next three and a half years was charted for me.

Epilogue

As I flew north in a BOAC Comet jet airliner in the middle of January 1963 (accompanied by Tony en route to his first term at Brighton College), I do not remember consciously thinking that my childhood had come to an end. My mind was seething with all the exciting possibilities that lay before me – six months in Paris at the Sorbonne to learn about the French culture and become fluent in their language, a pleasant summer in England renewing my acquaintance with English beer and playing lots of village cricket, and then who knew what inspiring and amazing experiences among the dreaming spires of England's most ancient university! Inevitably, though, I would have a new level of independence, a new range of decisions to make that would be up to me rather than my parents or some other 'responsible adult'. Like the country of my childhood, I had achieved a measure of self-government, and full independence was not far away!

And was this good-bye to Kenya? Well, no, that was delayed for another seven years!

My parents sold the Spring Valley house and packed up most of their belongings for shipment to Britain where, in due course, they were unloaded for storage in my grandmother's fortunately large garage at her home in Berkshire. They moved, temporarily it was said, into a guest cottage in the leafy and opulent Nairobi suburb of Muthaiga (they lived next door to the US Ambassador). But they never did actually get around to leaving Kenya. Ma died there in 1969 and Pa stayed on in the same cottage, looked after by the faithful Lasto, until he too took the one-way ticket to Paradise in 1978. They are buried next to each other in Langata cemetery just outside Nairobi.

Tony and I continued to come out to Kenya for holidays from school and university in the 1960s, always at least once, sometimes twice a year. After three happy years at Oxford, I joined the Commonwealth Development Corporation as a management trainee, and my first assignment with them was a short stint at the Tanganyika Wattle Company in the Southern Highlands of Tanzania, followed by two and a half years in the Regional Office in Nairobi. On my first return to Kenya after university I had enjoyed a belated 21st birthday celebration at the cottage in Muthaiga where I met for the first time a pretty girl of Anglo-Italian parentage called Shirley Jolley. Almost exactly three years later we were married at the Nairobi Cathedral and, six months after that left Kenya on postings to Swaziland and then Jamaica before migrating to Australia at the end of 1974. We made a fleeting return to Kenya from Swaziland at the end of 1971 for the christening of our first child, Tamsin. This was also supposed to take place in the Cathedral, but unfortunately Shirley came down with acute appendicitis and the venue was changed to the Nairobi Hospital Chapel. After the ceremony, she was wheeled away to the operating theatre to have the offending organ removed, and the rest of us went back to the Muthaiga cottage to drink champagne! I did spend a week back there in 1978 when Pa died, but otherwise our only return to the country since that time was a brief but very enjoyable holiday with Tony and his family in 1996.

I am sometimes asked what it was like, growing up in Africa. In some ways it was no different from growing up anywhere else. Whether you spend your childhood in the suburbs of a big city or a country town, in Europe, America, or Australia, much of what you face is the same: relationships with your parents, your siblings, your friends; coping with the often rapid changes in your mind and your body; learning all the strange and wonderful things about the world around you; dealing with triumphs and disappointments, happiness and misery.

The background to this common process, however, was, for me and my fellow colonials, unusual. The physical environment, for a start, was amazing. Kenya has an almost unique range of types of country, going from the dense tropical jungles in the high country, to the warm and humid forest at the coast with the wide, brown savannahs in between. There were places high enough and wet enough to grow tea and coffee, deserts where hardly anything would grow at all. There was snow, if you were willing and able to walk for long enough to get to it, and some of the world's most magical tropical beaches. Within this lived an extraordinary variety of beautiful creatures – brightly-coloured fish in the coral reefs at the coast, a profusion of animals of every imaginable kind from the mighty elephants to the slow and eye-swivelling chameleons, birds and butterflies of every size and colour. Even if you grew up mostly in an urban setting, as I did, the land and the creatures in it were an inevitable part of your existence.

The human element, too, was unusual. While the people with whom we were most intimately involved, our families, friends, school-fellows, were fairly homogeneous, we would also mix, to an increasing degree as time went on, with people of very different cultures. We commonly spoke, with varying degrees of fluency, a language other than our native tongue. Many urban communities in countries like Britain and Australia nowadays are multi-cultural, but we had in addition the growing realization that one of these (to us) alien cultures (the African) was destined, by sheer weight of numbers, to become dominant in the near future. It was something we had to come to terms with, a change undoubtedly easier for us than for our parents.

Looking back from more than half a century down my life's path, I can see many happy times, many wonderful experiences, few real regrets. In a sense, growing up in Kenya when I did prepared me for the world of change with which we are all having to cope. Kenya itself, from all I have observed, has changed greatly, perhaps mostly through the extraordinary population explosion that has occurred there, especially in the past 40 years. I will always, though, retain a deep affection for the land and its people and be very grateful for the fact that I was able to spend my formative years in such an astonishing place. Like all of us, I have played many roles in a longish and varied life. That of 'Bwana kidogo' was by no means the least rewarding of them!

Wedding at Nairobi Cathedral 1969 – my parents stand beside the happy couple and Best Man

About the Author

Chris Durrant was born in India to British parents in the last days of the Raj. He was brought up in Kenya, had three enjoyable and not completely wasted years at Oxford, and went back to East Africa to work for the Commonwealth Development Corporation (CDC), a sort of British equivalent of the World Bank. After postings with CDC in Swaziland and Jamaica, he migrated with his family to Australia. He now lives with his wife Shirley in the hills above Perth, Western Australia. Children and grandchildren are scattered around the world, including Perth.

Apart from financial management, Chris has worked as a pig farmer and a school-teacher. He is a rugby fanatic, an environmentalist, and a keen student of the history of the Great War, in which his father served and two of his uncles died. He has written his autobiography and a collection of whimsical essays about the school where he worked, as well as numerous songs and comic poems over the years. He has also co-authored several school accounting text-books. *Under the Same Moon*, his first novel, was published in 2018.

Find out more at: **chrisdurrant.com**
Or follow on Facebook: **facebook.com/ChrisDurrantauthor**

Printed in Great Britain
by Amazon

33158045R00097